AMERICA

JEAN BAUDRILLARD

VERSO

London • New York

First published as *Amérique* by Bernard Grasset, Paris 1986
This edition first published by Verso 2010
First published by Verso 1988
© Bernard Grasset 1986
© This translation Verso 1988
Introduction © Geoff Dyer 2010
All rights reserved

7 9 10 8

Verso
UK: 6 Meard Street, London W1F 0EG
US: 20 Jay Street, Suite 1010, Brooklyn, NY 11201
www.versobooks.com

Verso is the imprint of New Left Books

ISBN-13: 978-1-84467-682-8

British Library Cataloguing in Publication Data
A catalogue record for this book is available from the British Library

Library of Congress Cataloging-in-Publication Data
A catalog record for this book is available from the Library of Congress

Typeset by Hewer Text UK Ltd, Edinburgh
Printed and bound by CPI Group (UK) Ltd, Croydon, CR0 4YY

Contents

Translator's Acknowledgement

I would like to thank Dr Leslie Hill of the University of Warwick for his valuable assistance in preparing this translation.

Chris Turner

Introduction: Space and the Spirit of Fiction

When *America* was first published (in French in 1986, in English two years later) it seemed a book absolutely of its moment – a moment defined and shaped, in theory, by its author: super-star of the simulacrum, shaman of the virtual, evangelist of the hyperreal. It's often the fate of such fashionable works to fade quickly and disappear from view. Certainly, by the time of his death in 2007, Jean Baudrillard's reputation had been somewhat eclipsed, partly by the way that his thinking had been so thoroughly absorbed into the unauthored mind-set of post-modernity. *America*, though, is one of those rare works (Roland Barthes's *A Lover's Discourse* and *Camera Lucida* are others) to have escaped the ghetto of theory or cultural studies and established itself as a modern literary classic. In the pro-cess, naturally enough, its modishness has become less glaring and its place in a tradition more pronounced.

That tradition is a simple one, of Europeans – De Tocqueville, D. H. Lawrence, Sartre, Robert Frank – having a look around the United States and reporting back on what they see. No larger purpose is needed: the success of such trips depends on the quality of incidental observation, on a constant flux of sensations and ideas. Compiled on a beach in California (where, at night, people bathe 'like vampires, under the moonlight') or in the frenzy of Manhattan ('That life begins again each morning is a kind of miracle, considering how much energy was expended the day before'), *America* is a spectacular album of rhetorical postcards and road notes.

Simple though they are, these inverted versions of the Grand Tour tend, also, to double as a form of time travel, affording a view not only of what is going on in America (the New World, as it used to be called) but of what the future might hold for the rest of us, back in what Donald Rumsfeld charmingly christened 'old Europe'. The idea, as Frank put it in the application for the Guggenheim grant which would fund his mid-1950s road trip (and result in *The Americans*), is to observe 'the kind of civilization born here and spreading everywhere.'[1]

In keeping with – and updating – Frank's mission statement, Baudrillard arrived in San Diego in 1975 with 'the idea that California was a testing ground of simulation', only to find that 'this experimental side' was to be found 'in the deserts'.[2] The vast, arid expanses of the west (including the sprawling desert cities of Las Vegas and Los Angeles) became Baudrillard's heartland. Instead of 'historical or cultural comparison', the desert offered an absolute 'renunciation' or 'sweeping away' of culture.[3] As an ironic consequence the

1   Quoted in Belinda Rathbone, *Walker Evans: A Biography*, London: Thames and Hudson, 1995, p. 234.
2   Jean Baudrillard, *Paroxysm: Interviews with Philippe Petit*, London: Verso, 1998, p. 80.
3   *Paroxysm*, pp. 79, 81.

Parisian theorist was obliged to become a *nature* writer of visionary power. (Nature, it must be said, stripped of the very things – trees, fields, cows, hedges – which, in Europe, tend to constitute the natural.) The immense, geological silence of the American west has rarely been conveyed as vividly as in the passages recording Baudrillard's amazed reactions to the zero-humidity of Death Valley or the Mojave. 'The silence of the desert is a visual thing, too. A product of the gaze that stares out and finds nothing to reflect it. There can be no silence up in the mountains, since their very contours roar. And for there to be silence, time itself has to attain a sort of horizontality …'.

The ironies do not stop there, however. For Europeans, it turns out, have been culturally programmed to flourish in the culture-annihilating emptiness of the desert (Baudrillard's fashionable allure was enhanced by the covers of the English editions of his work, featuring images from Richard Misrach's ongoing 'Desert Cantos' series of photographs). To put it in Baudrillardian style, one could almost believe that the American deserts were created precisely in order to satisfy the cloud-stifled yearning of northern Europeans. The rejection of the 'civilized' in favour of the timeless and pre- and post-historic (or, if you prefer, pre- and post-human) desert was certainly what appealed to Lawrence. 'One forms not the faintest inward attachment,' he declared from New Mexico, in 1922. 'Only the desert has a fascination.'[4]

To help Baudrillard fathom his later fascination with and discovery of desertness, he occasionally consults Reyner Banham. In *Scenes in America Deserta,* Banham recounted

4   *Collected Letters, June 1921–March 1924,* Vol. IV, ed. Warren Roberts, James T. Boulton and Elizabeth Mansfield, Cambridge: Cambridge University Press, 1987, pp. 313–4.

what was for him the 'sensational discovery' of John C. Van Dyke's *The Desert* (1901).[5] Van Dyke was an art historian who, in 1898, travelled in the deserts of the southwest and saw, for the first time, that these desolate wastes comprised a hitherto unnoticed category of that most European of ideas – the sublime. Baudrillard leads back to Banham, who leads back to Van Dyke … Even in the desert, it turns out, a cultural trail has been pre-blazed and signposted. When Baudrillard discovers the 'fragment of another planet' that is Death Valley he is actually joining a procession of distinguished Europeans, including Michelangelo Antonioni (whose eponymous film climaxes at Zabriskie Point), and Michel Foucault who, in time-honoured fashion, dropped acid there. ('The sky has exploded and the stars are raining down upon me,' he said at the time. 'I know this is not true, but it is the Truth.')[6] All of these Europeans are drawn to Death Valley, of course, partly because of the American cultural capital amassed and derived from there, most famously the photographs made by Edward Weston who was 'so shaky with excitement' when he first went there in 1937 that he had trouble setting up his camera. 'My God!' he kept saying. 'It can't *be*.'[7]

A similar pattern – whereby the unmediated absolute turns out to be culturally determined – can be observed throughout the book. Baudrillard's brilliance is so intoxicating as to blind us to the people who prepared his mental map. The master of the paradox is himself its victim: things Baudrillard experiences as revelations have already been itemized by American

5   Cambridge, Mass.: MIT Press, 1989 [1982], p. 153.
6   Quoted by James Miller in *The Passion of Michel Foucault*, London: Harper Collins, 1993, p. 250.
7   Charis Wilson and Wendy Madar, *Through Another Lens: My Years with Edward Weston*, New York: North Point, 1998, p. 123.

artists who, by doing so, collapsed the oppositions on which he depends, between 'social and cultural America' on the one hand and 'absolute' or 'astral' America on the other. He recognizes that Monument Valley was created by John Huston and other directors of Westerns, but the 'marvellously affectless succession of signs, images, faces and ritual acts on the road' do not just *happen* to be there either; they have been staples of cultural life since Walker Evans and others surveyed and recorded them in the 1930s. In New York, when Baudrillard marvels at the 'people in the streets, wandering, carefree, violent, as if they had nothing better to do ... than produce the permanent scenario of the city' he is also paying tribute to the inexhaustible richness of Garry Winogrand's street scenes. Enthralled by 'the lack of culture' in a US he considers 'naive', Baudrillard urges us to 'embrace' this lack – an appeal that seems a little naive itself given that, since the Second World War at least, Americans have occupied the highest ground in every area of cultural endeavour. The days when America – as personified by Frank Wheeler in Richard Yates's *Revolutionary Road* – gazed longingly at the cultural supremacy and sophistication of Europe are long gone. The 'utopia achieved' in America is more thoroughgoing than even the admiring Baudrillard can quite bring himself to concede. In an interview he recalled that, during all his time in America, he 'never felt homesick for Europe':[8] a rare instance of Baudrillardian understatement, for in America Europe simply *disappears*.

As mentioned earlier, Baudrillard's observations of what is going on in America have a tacitly prophetic quality. But these State-of-the-Union pronouncements are themselves

8   *Paroxysm*, p. 83.

subject to cross-examination by the passage of time, high-
lighting the ways in which the oracular diagnosis was a
response to a place at a very particular point in its history.
Reading *America* now, in the wake of 9/11, in the aftermath
of the Obama election (to say nothing of Bush!), one is acutely
conscious that Baudrillard's America is also Reagan's; that
his New York predates Giuliani's Zero Tolerance make-over
of Manhattan; that AIDS had only just begun to imprint itself
on people's mental landscape; that the end of history was
about to be triumphantly – and, it turned out, misleadingly
– announced. And so on. This is not to say that the book
has dated (though the moment when the *philosophe* discovers the extraordinary 'feat of acrobatic gymnastics' called
'break-dancing' has come to seem rather quaint); it is to
situate the surge and swirl of Baudrillard's insights within a
larger history of cultural call and response – and, by so doing,
to qualify a few of his more extravagant claims.

Except, of course, the wildness is crucial to the book's
wit and sparkle, its exuberance and fun. To take issue with
Baudrillard's 'intellectual imperialism' in the affronted,
po-faced and flat-footed style of a Richard Poirier (see *Trying
it Out in America*) is to risk seeming a bit of a dullard.[9] There is
a certain style of writing that so clearly flaunts and delights in
its lack of moderation that readers, rather than objecting to or
stalling over a particular excess or silliness, willingly go with
the flow of slipstream exaggerations, heat-ripple visions and
switchback revelations. If it is 'imposture … make improbable

---

9   Richard Poirier, *Trying It Out in America*, New York: Farrar,
Straus and Giroux, 1999, Chapter 7. Naturally, I exempt from this Susan
Sontag's magisterial demolition of the idea that the Gulf War *only* existed
on TV as 'a breathtaking provincialism'. See *Regarding the Pain of Others*,
New York: Farrar Straus and Giroux, 2003, p. 110.

statements without appearing to do so, to stun people into silence with paradoxes', Baudrillard declares elsewhere, 'then long live imposture'.[10] *America*, by these terms, is a sustained and unrepentant display of authentic virtuoso imposture. (What most strikes him about the inferno of Death Valley is its '*mildness*', an observation which is ludicrous *and* entirely accurate: the intensity of heat and sun is such that all colours and features are muted, soft.)

Dizzyingly distinctive though it is, Baudrillard's style is, to a degree, culturally inherited. What Perry Anderson calls 'the formative role of rhetoric' is as crucial to Baudrillard as it was to the earlier generation of theorists – Barthes, Foucault, Lacan – who were also flamboyant (to their detractors, self-indulgent) stylists.[11] Barthes seems particularly close to Baudrillard, especially when he warns, at the outset of his book *Roland Barthes*, that 'all this must be considered as if spoken by a character in a novel.'[12]

The penultimate section of America ends with a brief reflection on 'space and the spirit of fiction'. Looking back on his time in the States, Baudrillard reflected on the way that 'over there, even theory becomes once again what it is: a fiction.'[13] That's exactly what happens in America: a Euro distillation of American fiction – without the narrative bulk.

Here is Don DeLillo from *Americana*:

10　Jean Baudrillard, *Cool Memories IV, 1995–2000*, London: Verso, 2003, p. 52.
11　Perry Anderson, *The New Old World*, London: Verso, 2009, p. 143.
12　Roland Barthes, *Roland Barthes*, New York: Farrar, Straus and Giroux, p. 119.
13　*Paroxysm*, p. 82.

Repeated endlessly on the way to your room, you can easily forget who you are here; you can sit on your bed and become man sitting on bed, an abstraction to compete with infinity itself; out of such places and moments does modern chaos raise itself to the level of pure mathematics. Despite its great size, the motel seems temporary ... There are too many hangers in the closet, as if management were trying to compensate for a secret insufficiency too grievous to be imagined. From small gratings in the wall comes a steady and almost unendurable whisper of ventilation. But for all its spiritual impoverishments, this isn't the worst of places. It embodies a repetition so insistent and irresistible that, if not freedom, then liberation is possible, deliverance; possessed by chaos, you move into thinner realms, achieve refinements, mathematical integrity, and become, if you choose, the man on the bed in the next room.[14]

Here is Baudrillard from *America*:

There is nothing more mysterious than a TV set left on in an empty room ... Suddenly the TV reveals itself for what it really is: a video of another world, ultimately addressed to no one at all, delivering its images indifferently, indifferent to its own messages (you can easily imagine it still functioning after humanity has disappeared).

Here we have the ultimate fascination of *America*: the chance to see what might happen if an American novelist assumed the form of a great French theorist; or, to put it the other way around, what might happen if Baudrillard reinvented himself as a great American novelist.

14   New York: Penguin, 1989 [1971], p. 257.

Vanishing Point

Caution: Objects in this mirror may be closer than they appear!

Nostalgia born of the immensity of the Texan hills and the sierras of New Mexico: gliding down the freeway, smash hits on the Chrysler stereo, heat wave. Snapshots aren't enough. We'd need the whole film of the trip in real time, including the unbearable heat and the music. We'd have to replay it all from end to end at home in a darkened room, rediscover the magic of the freeways and the distance and the ice-cold alcohol in the desert and the speed and live it all again on the video at home in real time, not simply for the pleasure of remembering but because the fascination of senseless repetition is already present in the abstraction of the journey. The unfolding of the desert is infinitely close to the timelessness of film . . .

San Antonio

The Mexicans, become Chicanos, act as guides on the visit to El Alamo to laud the heroes of the American nation so valiantly massacred by their own ancestors. But hard as those ancestors fought, the division of labour won out in the end.

Today it is their grandchildren and great-grandchildren who
are there, on the same battlefield, to hymn the Americans
who stole their lands. History is full of ruse and cunning. But
so are the Mexicans who have crossed the border clandes-
tinely to come and work here.

Salt Lake City

Pompous Mormon symmetry. Everywhere marble: flaw-
less, funereal (the Capitol, the organ in the Visitor Center).
Yet a Los-Angelic modernity, too – all the requisite
gadgetry for a minimalist, extraterrestrial comfort. The
Christ-topped dome (all the Christs here are copied from
Thorwaldsen's and look like Björn Borg) straight out of
Close Encounters: religion as special effects. In fact the whole
city has the transparency and supernatural, otherworldly
cleanness of a thing from outer space. A symmetrical,
luminous, overpowering abstraction. At every intersection
in the Tabernacle area – all marble and roses, and evan-
gelical marketing – an electronic cuckoo-clock sings out:
such Puritan obsessiveness is astonishing in this heat, in
the heart of the desert, alongside this leaden lake, its waters
also hyperreal from sheer density of salt. And, beyond the
lake, the Great Salt Lake Desert, where they had to invent
the speed of prototype cars to cope with the absolute horizontality . . . But the city itself is like a jewel, with its purity
of air and its plunging urban vistas more breathtaking even
than those of Los Angeles. What stunning brilliance, what
modern veracity these Mormons show, these rich bank-
ers, musicians, international genealogists, polygamists (the
Empire State in New York has something of this same funereal Puritanism raised to the nth power). It is the capitalist,

transsexual pride of a people of mutants that gives the city its magic, equal and opposite to that of Las Vegas, that great whore on the other side of the desert.

Monument Valley
Dead Horse Point
Grand Canyon

Geological – and hence metaphysical – monumentality, by contrast with the physical altitude of ordinary landscapes. Upturned relief patterns, sculpted out by wind, water, and ice, dragging you down into the whirlpool of time, into the remorseless eternity of a slow-motion catastrophe. The very idea of the millions and hundreds of millions of years that were needed peacefully to ravage the surface of the earth here is a perverse one, since it brings with it an awareness of signs originating, long before man appeared, in a sort of pact of wear and erosion struck between the elements. Among this gigantic heap of signs – purely geological in essence – man will have had no significance. The Indians alone perhaps interpreted them – a few of them. And yet they *are* signs. For the desert only *appears* uncultivated. This entire Navajo country, the long plateau which leads to the Grand Canyon, the cliffs overlooking Monument Valley, the abysses of Green River are all alive with a magical presence, which has nothing to do with nature (the secret of this whole stretch of country is perhaps that it was once an underwater relief and has retained the surrealist qualities of an ocean bed in the open air). You can understand why it took great magic on the Indians' part, and a terribly cruel religion, to exorcize such a theoretical grandeur as the desert's geological and celestial occurrence, to live up to such a backdrop. What is man if the signs that predate him have such power? A human race has to invent sacrifices equal to the natural cataclysmic order that surrounds it.

It is perhaps these reliefs, because they are no longer natural, which give the best idea of what a culture is. Monument Valley: blocks of language suddenly rising high, then subjected to a pitiless erosion, ancient sedimentations that owe their depth to wear (meaning is born out of the erosion of words, significations are born out of the erosion of signs), and that are today destined to become, like all that is cultivated – like all culture – natural parks.

SALT LAKE CITY: the world genealogical archives, presided over in the depths of the desert caves by those rich-living, puritanical conquistadors, the Mormons, and, alongside, the Bonneville track on the immaculate surface of the Great Salt Lake Desert, where prototype cars achieve the highest speeds in the world. Patronymic genesis as the depth of time, and the speed of sound as pure superficiality.

ALAMOGORDO: the first atomic-bomb test against the backdrop of White Sands, the pale blue backcloth of the mountains and hundreds of miles of white sand – the blinding artificial light of the bomb against the blinding light of the ground.

TORREY CANYON: the Salk Institute, sanctuary of DNA and all the Nobel Prize winners for biology. There all the future biological commandments are being devised, within that architecture copied from the palace of Minos, its white marble staring out over the immensity of the Pacific . . .

Extraordinary sites, capitals of fiction become reality. Sublime, transpolitical sites of extraterritoriality, combining as they do the earth's undamaged geological grandeur with a sophisticated, nuclear, orbital, computer technology.

I went in search of *astral* America*, not social and cultural America, but the America of the empty, absolute freedom of the freeways, not the deep America of mores and mentalities, but the America of desert speed, of motels and mineral surfaces. I looked for it in the speed of the screenplay, in the indifferent reflex of television, in the film of days and nights projected across an empty space, in the marvellously affectless succession of signs, images, faces, and ritual acts on the road; looked for what was nearest to the nuclear and enucleated universe, a universe which is virtually our own, right down to its European cottages.

I sought the finished form of the future catastrophe of the social in geology, in that upturning of depth that can be seen in the striated spaces, the reliefs of salt and stone, the canyons where the fossil river flows down, the immemorial abyss of slowness that shows itself in erosion and geology. I even looked for it in the verticality of the great cities.

I knew all about this nuclear form, this future catastrophe when I was still in Paris, of course. But to understand it, you have to take to the road, to that travelling which achieves what Virilio calls the aesthetics of disappearance.

For the mental desert form expands before your very eyes, and this is the purified form of social desertification. Disaffection finds its pure form in the barrenness of speed. All that is cold and dead in desertification or social enucleation rediscovers its contemplative form here in the heat of the desert. Here in the transversality of the desert and the irony

* 'l'Amérique sidérale': this term and its variant forms have been rendered throughout by 'astral' or the less familiar 'sidereal', according to context. [Tr.]

of geology, the transpolitical finds its generic, mental space. The inhumanity of our ulterior, asocial, superficial world immediately finds its aesthetic form here, its ecstatic form. For the desert is simply that: an ecstatic critique of culture, an ecstatic form of disappearance.

The grandeur of deserts derives from their being, in their aridity, the negative of the earth's surface and of our civilized humours. They are places where humours and fluids become rarefied, where the air is so pure that the influence of the stars descends direct from the constellations. And, with the extermination of the desert Indians, an even earlier stage than that of anthropology became visible: a mineralogy, a geology, a sidereality, an inhuman facticity, an aridity that drives out the artificial scruples of culture, a silence that exists nowhere else.

The silence of the desert is a visual thing, too. A product of the gaze that stares out and finds nothing to reflect it. There can be no silence up in the mountains, since their very contours roar. And for there to be silence, time itself has to attain a sort of horizontality; there has to be no echo of time in the future, but simply a sliding of geological strata one upon the other giving out nothing more than a fossil murmur.

Desert: luminous, fossilized network of an inhuman intelligence, of a radical indifference – the indifference not merely of the sky, but of the geological undulations, where the metaphysical passions of space and time alone crystallize. Here the terms of desire are turned upside down each day, and night annihilates them. But wait for the dawn to rise, with the awakening of the fossil sounds, the animal silence.

Speed creates pure objects. It is itself a pure object, since it cancels out the ground and territorial reference-points, since it runs ahead of time to annul time itself, since it moves more quickly than its own cause and obliterates that cause by outstripping it. Speed is the triumph of effect over cause, the triumph of instantaneity over time as depth, the triumph of the surface and pure objectality over the profundity of desire. Speed creates a space of initiation, which may be lethal; its only rule is to leave no trace behind. Triumph of forgetting over memory, an uncultivated, amnesic intoxication. The superficiality and reversibility of a pure object in the pure geometry of the desert. Driving like this produces a kind of invisibility, transparency, or transversality in things, simply by emptying them out. It is a sort of slow-motion suicide, death by an extenuation of forms – the delectable form of their disappearance. Speed is not a vegetal thing. It is nearer to the mineral, to refraction through a crystal, and it is already the site of a catastrophe, of a squandering of time. Perhaps, though, its fascination is simply that of the void. There is no seduction here, for seduction requires a secret. Speed is simply the rite that initiates us into emptiness: a nostalgic desire for forms to revert to immobility, concealed beneath the very intensification of their mobility. Akin to the nostalgia for living forms that haunts geometry.

Still, there is a violent contrast here, in this country, between the growing abstractness of a nuclear universe and a primary, visceral, unbounded vitality, springing not from rootedness, but from the lack of roots, a metabolic vitality, in sex and bodies, as well as in work and in buying and selling. Deep down, the US, with its space, its technological refinement, its bluff good conscience, even in those spaces which it opens up for simulation, is the *only remaining primitive society*. The fascinating thing is to travel through it as though it were the primitive society of the future, a society of complexity, hybridity, and the greatest intermingling, of a ritualism that is ferocious but whose superficial diversity lends it beauty, a society inhabited by a total metasocial fact with unforeseeable consequences, whose immanence is breathtaking, yet lacking a past through which to reflect on this, and therefore fundamentally primitive . . . Its primitivism has passed into the hyperbolic, inhuman character of a universe that is beyond us, that far outstrips its own moral, social, or ecological rationale.

Only Puritans could have invented and developed this ecological and biological morality based on preservation – and therefore on discrimination – which is profoundly racial in nature. Everything becomes an overprotected nature reserve, so protected indeed that there is talk today of denaturalizing Yosemite to give it back to Nature, as has happened with the Tasaday in the Philippines. A Puritan obsession with origins in the very place where the ground itself has already gone. An obsession with finding a niche, a contact, precisely at the point where everything unfolds in an astral indifference.

There is a sort of miracle in the insipidity of *artificial paradises*, so long as they achieve the greatness of an entire (un) culture. In America, space lends a sense of grandeur even to the insipidity of the suburbs and 'funky towns'. The desert is everywhere, preserving insignificance. A desert where the miracle of the car, of ice and whisky is daily re-enacted: a marvel of easy living mixed with the fatality of the desert. A miracle of obscenity that is genuinely American: a miracle of total availability, of the transparency of all functions in space, though this latter nonetheless remains unfathomable in its vastness and can only be exorcised by speed.

The Italian miracle: that of stage and scene.

The American miracle: that of the obscene.

The profusion of sense, as against the deserts of meaninglessness.

It is metamorphic forms that are magical. Not the sylvan, vegetal forest, but the petrified, mineralized forest. The salt desert, whiter than snow, flatter than the sea. The effect of monumentality, geometry, and architecture where nothing has been designed or planned. Canyonsland, Split Mountain. Or the opposite: the amorphous reliefless relief of Mud Hills, the voluptuous, fossilized, monotonously undulating lunar relief of ancient lake beds. The white swell of White Sands . . . It takes this surreality of the elements to eliminate nature's picturesque qualities, just as it takes the metaphysics of speed to eliminate the natural picturesqueness of travel.

In fact the conception of a trip without any objective and which is, as a result, endless, only develops gradually for me. I reject the picturesque tourist round, the sights, even the landscapes (only their abstraction remains, in the prism of the scorching heat). Nothing is further from pure travelling than tourism or holiday travel. That is why it is best done in the extensive banality of deserts, or in the equally desert-like banality of a metropolis – not at any stage regarded as places of pleasure or culture, but seen televisually as scenery, as scenarios. That is why it is best done in extreme heat, the orgasmic form of bodily deterritorialization. The acceleration of molecules in the heat contributes to a barely perceptible evaporation of meaning.

It is not the discovery of local customs that counts, but discovering the immorality of the space you have to travel through, and this is on a quite different plane. It is this,

together with the sheer distance, and the deliverance from
the social, that count. Here in the most moral society there
is, space is truly immoral. Here in the most conformist society, the dimensions are immoral. It is this immorality that
makes distance light and the journey infinite, that cleanses
the muscles of their tiredness.

Driving is a spectacular form of amnesia. Everything is to be
discovered, everything to be obliterated. Admittedly, there is
the primal shock of the deserts and the dazzle of California,
but when this is gone, the secondary brilliance of the journey begins, that of the excessive, pitiless distance, the infinity
of anonymous faces and distances, or of certain miraculous
geological formations, which ultimately testify to no human
will, while keeping intact an image of upheaval. This form
of travel admits of no exceptions: when it runs up against
a known face, a familiar landscape, or some decipherable
message, the spell is broken: the amnesic, ascetic, asymp-
totic charm of disappearance succumbs to affect and worldly
semiology.

   This sort of travel creates its own peculiar type of event
and innervation, so it also has its own special form of fatigue.
Like a fibrillation of muscles, striated by the excess of heat
and speed, by the excess of things seen or read, of places
passed through and forgotten. The defibrillation of the body
overloaded with empty signs, functional gestures, the blinding brilliance of the sky, and somnambulistic distances, is
a very slow process. Things suddenly become lighter, as
culture, our culture, becomes more rarefied. And this spectral
form of civilization which the Americans have invented, an
ephemeral form so close to vanishing point, suddenly seems
the best adapted to the probability – the probability only – of

the life that lies in store for us. The form that dominates the American West, and doubtless all of American culture, is a seismic form: a fractal, interstitial culture, born of a rift with the Old World, a tactile, fragile, mobile, superficial culture – you have to follow its own rules to grasp how it works: seismic shifting, soft technologies.

The only question in this journey is: how far can we go in the extermination of meaning, how far can we go in the non-referential desert form without cracking up and, of course, still keep alive the esoteric charm of disappearance? A theoretical question here materialized in the objective conditions of a journey which is no longer a journey and therefore carries with it a fundamental rule: aim for the point of no return. This is the key. And the crucial moment is that brutal instant which reveals that the journey has no end, that there is no longer any reason for it to come to an end. Beyond a certain point, it is movement itself that changes. Movement which moves through space of its own volition changes into an absorption by space itself – end of resistance, end of the scene of the journey as such (exactly as the jet engine is no longer an energy of space-penetration, but propels itself by creating a vaccum in front of it that sucks it forward, instead of supporting itself, as in the traditional model, upon the air's resistance). In this way, the centrifugal, eccentric point is reached where movement produces the vacuum that sucks you in. This moment of vertigo is also the moment of potential collapse. Not so much from the tiredness generated by the distance and the heat, as from the irreversible advance into the desert of time.

Tomorrow is the first day of the rest of your life.

New York

Aeronautic missionary of the silent majorities, I jump with cat-like tread from one airport to the other. Now it's the blazing woods of New Hampshire, casting a fleeting reflection in the mirror of New England. Yesterday, it was the steepling gentleness of skyscrapers. Tomorrow it will be Minneapolis with its sweet-sounding name, its gossamer string of vowels, half-Greek, half-Cheyenne, evoking a radiating geometric pattern, at the edge of the ice-sheets, at the horizon of the inhabited world . . . Speaking of the silence of the masses and the end of history, and casting an eye over the immensity and radiance of the lake. A biting wind blows over it, away to the east where night is falling. Planes pass overhead, silent as the wind, behind the windowpanes of the hotel, and the first neon signs begin to roll slowly, above the city. What an amazing place America is! All around is Indian summer, its mildness presaging snow. But where are the ten thousand lakes, the utopian dream of a Hellenistic city on the edge of the Rockies? Minneapolis, Minneapolis! After the patrician elegance and feminine gentleness of the Indian summer in Wisconsin, Minneapolis is merely a rural agglomeration, simply waiting in darkness amid its silos and hunting grounds for the winter and the cold on which it prides itself. But in the depths of this real America, there is the Commodore bar, with the finest art deco in the world, where Fitzgerald, they say, drank every evening. I drink there too. Tomorrow I shall be carried directly by plane to the opposite extreme, opposite in terms of light, surface area, racial mix, aesthetics, and power – to the city that is heir to all other cities at once. Heir to Athens, Alexandria, Persepolis: New York.

New York

More sirens here, day and night. The cars are faster, the advertisements more aggressive. This is wall-to-wall prostitution. And total electric light too. And the game – all games – gets more intense. It's always like this when you're getting near the centre of the world. But the people smile. Actually they smile more and more, though never to other people, always to themselves.

The terrifying diversity of faces, their strangeness, strained as they all are into unbelievable expressions. The masks old age or death conferred in archaic cultures are worn here by youngsters of twenty or twelve. But this reflects the city as a whole. The beauty other cities only acquired over centuries has been achieved by New York in fifty years.

Plumes of smoke, reminiscent of girls wringing out their hair after bathing. Afro or pre-Raphaelite hairstyles. Run-of-the-mill, multiracial. City of Pharaohs, all obelisks and needles. The blocks around Central Park are like flying buttresses, lending the huge park the appearance of a hanging garden.

It isn't clouds that are fleecy here, but brains. Clouds float over the city like cerebral hemispheres driven by the wind.

The people have cirrus clouds in their heads or coming out of their eyes, like the spongy vapours that rise from earth cracked by hot rains. Sexual solitude of clouds in the sky; linguistic solitude of men on the earth.

The number of people here who think alone, sing alone, and eat and talk alone in the streets is mind-boggling. And yet they don't add up. Quite the reverse. They subtract from each other and their resemblance to one another is uncertain.

Yet there is a certain solitude like no other – that of the man preparing his meal in public on a wall, or on the hood of his car, or along a fence, alone. You see that all the time here. It is the saddest sight in the world. Sadder than destitution, sadder than the beggar is the man who eats alone in public. Nothing more contradicts the laws of man or beast, for animals always do each other the honour of sharing or disputing each other's food. He who eats alone is dead (but not he who drinks alone. Why is this?).

Why do people live in New York? There is no relationship between them. Except for an inner electricity which results from the simple fact of their being crowded together. A magical sensation of contiguity and attraction for an artificial centrality. This is what makes it a self-attracting universe, which there is no reason to leave. There is no human reason to be here, except for the sheer ecstasy of being crowded together.

The beauty of the Black and Puerto Rican women of New York. Apart from the sexual stimulation produced by the crowding together of so many races, it must be said that black, the pigmentation of the dark races, is like a natural make-up that is set off by the artificial kind to produce a beauty which is not sexual, but sublime and animal – a beauty which the pale faces so desperately lack. Whiteness seems an extenuation of physical adornment, a neutrality which, perhaps by that very token, claims all the exoteric powers of the Word, but ultimately will never possess the esoteric and ritual potency of artifice.

In New York there is this double miracle: each of the great buildings and each of the ethnic groups dominates or has dominated the city – after its own fashion. Here crowdedness lends sparkle to each of the ingredients in the mix whereas elsewhere it tends to cancel out differences. In Montreal, all the same elements are present – ethnic groups, buildings, and space on the grand American scale – but the sparkle and violence of American cities are missing.

Clouds spoil our European skies. Compared with the immense skies of America and their thick clouds, our little fleecy skies and little fleecy clouds resemble our fleecy thoughts, which are never thoughts of wide open spaces . . . In Paris, the sky never takes off. It doesn't soar above us. It remains caught up in the backdrop of sickly buildings, all living in each other's shade, as though it were a little piece of private property. It is not, as here in the great capital New York, the vertiginous glass facade reflecting each building to the others. Europe has never been a continent. You can see that by its skies. As soon as you set foot in America, you feel the presence of an entire continent – space there is the very form of thought.

By contrast with the American 'downtown areas' and their blocks of skyscrapers, la Défense has forfeited the archi-tectural benefits of verticality and excess by squeezing its

high-rise blocks into an Italian-style setting, into a closed
theatre bounded by a ring-road. It is very much a garden
à la française: a bunch of buildings with a ribbon around
it. All this has closed off the possibility that these monsters
might engender others to infinity, that they might battle it
out within a space rendered dramatic by their very competition (New York, Chicago, Houston, Seattle, Toronto). It
is in such a space that the pure architectural object is born,
an object beyond the control of architects, which roundly
repudiates the city and its uses, repudiates the interests of the
collectivity and individuals and persists in its own madness.
That object has no equivalent, except perhaps the arrogance
of the cities of the Renaissance.

No, architecture should not be humanized. Anti-architecture,
the true sort (not the kind you find in Arcosanti, Arizona,
which gathers together all the 'soft' technologies in the heart
of the desert), the wild, inhuman type that is beyond the meas-
ure of man was made here – made itself here – in New York,
without considerations of setting, well-being, or ideal ecology.
It opted for hard technologies, exaggerated all dimensions,
gambled on heaven and hell . . . Eco-architecture, eco-society
. . . this is the gentle hell of the Roman Empire in its decline.

Modern demolition is truly wonderful. As a spectacle it is the
opposite of a rocket launch. The twenty-storey block remains
perfectly vertical as it slides towards the centre of the earth. It
falls straight, with no loss of its upright bearing, like a tailor's
dummy falling through a trap-door, and its own surface area
absorbs the rubble. What a marvellous modern art form this
is, a match for the firework displays of our childhood.

* * *

They say the streets are alive in Europe, but dead in America. They are wrong. Nothing could be more intense, electrifying, turbulent, and vital than the streets of New York. They are filled with crowds, bustle, and advertisements, each by turns aggressive or casual. There are millions of people in the streets, wandering, carefree, violent, as if they had nothing better to do – and doubtless they have nothing else to do – than produce the permanent scenario of the city. There is music everywhere; the activity is intense, relatively violent, and silent (it is not the agitated, theatrical activity you find in Italy). The streets and avenues never empty, but the neat, spacious geometry of the city is far removed from the thronging intimacy of the narrow streets of Europe.

In Europe, the street only lives in sudden surges, in historic moments of revolution and barricades. At other times people move along briskly, no one really hangs around (no one wanders any more). It is the same with European cars. No one actually lives in them; there isn't enough space. The cities, too, do not have enough space, or rather that space is deemed public and bears all the marks of the public arena, which forbids you to cross it or wander around it as though it were a desert or some indifferent area.

The American street has not, perhaps, known these historic moments, but it is always turbulent, lively, kinetic, and cinematic, like the country itself, where the specifically historical and political stage counts for little, but where change, whether spurred by technology, racial differences, or the media, assumes virulent forms: its violence is the very violence of the way of life.

Such is the whirl of the city, so great its centrifugal force, that it would take superhuman strength to envisage living as a couple and sharing someone else's life in New York. Only tribes, gangs, mafia families, secret societies, and perverse communities can survive, not couples. This is the anti-Ark. In the first Ark, the animals came in two by two to save the species from the great flood. Here in this fabulous Ark, each one comes in alone – it's up to him or her each evening to find the last survivors for the last party.

In New York, the mad have been set free. Let out into the city, they are difficult to tell apart from the rest of the punks, junkies, addicts, winos, or down-and-outs who inhabit it. It is difficult to see why a city as crazy as this one would keep its mad in the shadows, why it would withdraw from circulation specimens of a madness which has in fact, in its various forms, taken hold of the whole city.

'Breakdancing' is a feat of acrobatic gymnastics. Only at the end do you realize it actually was dancing, when the dancer freezes into a lazy, languid pose (elbow on the ground, head nonchalantly resting in the palm of the hand, the pose you see on Etruscan tombs). The way they suddenly come to rest like this is reminiscent of Chinese opera. But the Chinese warrior comes to a halt at the height of the action in a heroic gesture, whereas the breakdancer stops at the slack point in his movements and the gesture is derisive. You might say that in curling up and spiralling around on the ground like this, they seem to be digging a hole for themselves within their own bodies, from which to stare out in the ironic, indolent pose of the dead.

I would never have believed that the New York marathon could move you to tears. It really is the end-of-the-world show. Can we speak of suffering freely entered into as we might speak of a state of servitude freely entered into? In driving rain, with helicopters circling overhead and the crowd cheering, wearing aluminium foil capes and squinting at their stop-watches, or bare-chested, their eyes rolling skywards, they are all seeking death, that death by exhaustion that was the fate of the first Marathon man some two thousand years ago. And he, let us not forget, was carrying a message of victory to Athens. They also dream no doubt of bringing a victory message, but there are too many of them and their message has lost all meaning: it is merely the message of their arrival, at the end of their exertions, the twilight message of a futile, superhuman effort. Collectively, they might rather seem to be bringing the message of a catastrophe for the human race, which you can see becoming more and more decrepit by the hour as the runners come in, from the competitive, athletic types who arrive first to the wrecks who are literally carried to the finishing line by their friends, or the handicapped who do the race in their wheelchairs. There are 17,000 runners and you can't help thinking back to the Battle of Marathon, where there weren't even 17,000 soldiers in the field. There are 17,000 of them and each one runs alone, without even a thought for victory, but simply in order to feel alive. 'We won', gasped the man from Marathon as he expired. 'I did it!', sighs the exhausted marathon runner of New York as he collapses on the grass in Central Park.

I Did It!

The slogan of a new form of advertising activity, of autistic performance, a pure and empty form, a challenge to one's own self that has replaced the Promethean ecstasy of competition, effort, and success.

The New York marathon has become a sort of international symbol of such fetishistic performance, of the mania for an empty victory, the joy engendered by a feat that is of no consequence.

I ran the New York marathon: 'I did it!'

I conquered Annapurna: 'I did it!'

The moon landing is the same kind of thing: 'We did it!' The event was ultimately not really so surprising; it was an event pre-programmed into the course of science and progress. We did it. But it has not revived the millenarian dream of conquering space. In a sense, it has exhausted it.

Carrying out any kind of programme produces the same sense of futility that comes from doing anything merely to prove to yourself that you can do it: having a child, climbing a mountain, making some sexual conquest, committing suicide.

The marathon is a form of demonstrative suicide, suicide as advertising: it is running to show you are capable of getting every last drop of energy out of yourself, to prove it . . . to prove what? That you are capable of finishing. Graffiti carry the same message. They simply say: I'm so-and-so and I exist! They are free publicity for existence.

Do we continually have to prove to ourselves that we exist? A strange sign of weakness, harbinger of a new fanaticism for a faceless performance, endlessly self-evident.

Mystic Transportation Incorporated

A blue-green lorry with gleaming chromework is going down Seventh Avenue in the early morning sun, just after a snowfall. It bears on its sides, in gold metallic lettering, the words 'Mystic Transportation'.

It sums up the whole of New York and its mystical view of decadence. Every special effect can be found here, from sublime verticality to decay on the ground, all the special effects of the mixing of races and empires. This is the fourth dimension of the city.

In years to come cities will stretch out horizontally and will be non-urban (Los Angeles). After that, they will bury themselves in the ground and will no longer even have names. Everything will become infrastructure bathed in artificial light and energy. The brilliant superstructure, the crazy verticality will have disappeared. New York is the final fling of this baroque verticality, this centrifugal excentricity, before the horizontal dismantling arrives, and the subterranean implosion that will follow.

With the marvellous complicity of its entire population, New York acts out its own catastrophe as a stage play. And this is not an effect of its decadence, but of its own power, to which there is, of course, no threat. In fact, this absence of threat is its power. Its density, its surface electricity rule out any thought of war. That life begins again each morning is a kind of miracle, considering how much energy was expended the day before. Its voltage protects it, like a galvanic dome, from all external threats – though not from internal accidents like the black-out of '76. Yet the scale of these makes them world events and simply adds further to the city's glory. This centrality and eccentricity can only create a crazed sense of its own end, which the New York 'scene' aesthetically transcribes in its follies and its violent expressionism, and which the whole city collectively cultivates in its technical frenzy for the vertical, its constant acceleration of the banal, the liveliness of its faces, whether happy or wretched, and the insolence of its sacrifice of humans to pure circulation.

No one looks at you, caught up as they all are in their passionate efforts to carry off their own impersonal roles. There are no cops in New York – elsewhere they are there to give a modern, urban look to cities that are still semi-rural (Paris is a good example). Here, urbanization has reached such a pitch that there is no longer any need to express it or give it a political character. Anyway, New York is no longer a political city and demonstrations by its various ideological groups are rare and invariably derisory (the ethnic groups express themselves through festivals and the racial demonstration of their presence). New York's violence is not a violence of social relations, but of *all relations*, and it is exponential. Sexuality itself has to some extent been left behind as a form of expression. Even though it is everywhere on display, it no longer has the time to realize itself in human love-relationships. It evaporates into the promiscuity of each passing moment, into a multiplicity of more ephemeral forms of contact. You rediscover a feeling of glory in New York, in the sense that you feel wreathed in the general energy of the place – what you are part of here is not the lugubrious spectacle of change, as you find it in Europe, but the aesthetic form of a mutation.

We in Europe possess the art of thinking, of analysing things and reflecting on them. No one disputes our historical subtlety and conceptual imagination. Even the great minds across the Atlantic envy us in this regard. But the resounding truths, the realities of genuinely great moment today are to be found along the Pacific seaboard or in Manhattan. It has to be said that New York and Los Angeles are at the centre of the world, even if we find the idea somehow both exciting and disenchanting. We are a desperately long way behind the stupidity and the mutational character, the naive extravagance and the social, racial, moral, morphological, and architectural excentricity of their society. No one is capable of analysing it, least of all the American intellectuals shut away on their campuses, dramatically cut off from the fabulous concrete mythology developing all around them.

It is a world completely rotten with wealth, power, senility, indifference, puritanism and mental hygiene, poverty and waste, technological futility and aimless violence, and yet I cannot help but feel it has about it something of the dawning of the universe. Perhaps because the entire world continues to dream of New York, even as New York dominates and exploits it.

At 30,000 feet and 600 miles per hour, I have beneath me the ice-floes of Greenland, the *Indes Galantes* in my earphones, Catherine Deneuve on the screen, and an old man – a Jew or an Armenian – asleep on my lap. 'Yes, I feel all the violence of love . . .' sings the sublime voice, from one time zone to the next. The people in the plane are asleep. Speed knows nothing of the violence of love. Between one night and the next, the one we came from and the one we shall land in, there will have been only four hours daylight. But the sublime voice, the voice of insomnia travels even more quickly. It moves through the freezing, trans-oceanic atmosphere, runs along the long lashes of the actress, along the horizon, violet where the sun is rising, as we fly along in our warm coffin of a jet, and finally fades away somewhere off the coast of Iceland.

The journey is over.

Astral America

Astral America. The lyrical nature of pure circulation. As against the melancholy of European analyses. The direct star-blast from vectors and signals, from the vertical and the spatial. As against the fevered distance of the cultural gaze.

Joy in the collapse of metaphor, which here in Europe we merely grieve over. The exhilaration of obscenity, the obscenity of obviousness, the obviousness of power, the power of simulation. As against our disappointed virginity, our chasms of affectation.

Sideration. Star-blasted, horizontally by the car, altitudinally by the plane, electronically by television, geologically by deserts, stereolithically by the megalopoloi, transpolitically by the power game, the power museum that America has become for the whole world.

For me there is no truth of America. I ask of the Americans only that they be Americans. I do not ask them to be intelligent, sensible, original. I ask them only to populate a space incommensurate with my own, to be for me the highest astral point, the finest orbital space. Why should I go and decentralize myself in France, in the ethnic and the local, which are merely the shreds and vestiges of centrality? I want to excentre myself, to become eccentric, but I want to do so in a place that is the centre of the world. And, in this sense, the latest fast-food outlet, the most banal suburb, the blandest of giant American cars or the most insignificant cartoon-strip majorette is more at the centre of the world than any of the cultural manifestations of old Europe. This is the only country which gives you the opportunity to be so brutally naive: things, faces, skies, and deserts are expected to be simply what they are. This is the land of the 'just as it is'.

America always gives me a feeling of real asceticism. Culture, politics – and sexuality too – are seen exclusively in terms of the desert, which here assumes the status of a primal scene. Everything disappears before that desert vision. Even the body, by an ensuing effect of undernourishment, takes on a transparent form, a lightness near to complete disappearance. Everything around me suffers this same desertification. But this radical experimentation is the only thing that enables me to get through and produces that astral quality I have not found anywhere else.

America is neither dream nor reality. It is a hyperreality. It is a hyperreality because it is a utopia which has behaved from the very beginning as though it were already achieved. Everything here is real and pragmatic, and yet it is all the stuff of dreams too. It may be that the truth of America can only be seen by a European, since he alone will discover here the perfect simulacrum – that of the immanence and material transcription of all values. The Americans, for their part, have no sense of simulation. They are themselves simulation in its most developed state, but they have no language in which to describe it, since they themselves are the model. As a result, they are the ideal material for an analysis of all the possible variants of the modern world. No more and no less in fact than were primitive societies in their day. The same mythical and analytic excitement that made us look towards those earlier societies today impels us to look in the direction of America. With the same passion and the same prejudices.

In reality, you do not, as I had hoped, get any distance on Europe from here. You do not acquire a fresh angle on it. When you turn around, it has quite simply disappeared. The point is that there is really no need to adopt a critical stance on Europe from here. That is something you can do in Europe. And what is there to criticize which has not been criticized a thousand times before? What you have to do is enter the fiction of America, enter America as fiction. It is, indeed, on this fictive basis that it dominates the world. Even if every detail of America were insignificant, America is something that is beyond us all . . .

America is a giant hologram, in the sense that information concerning the whole is contained in each of its elements. Take the tiniest little place in the desert, any old street in a Midwestern town, a parking lot, a Californian house, a Burger King or a Studebaker, and you have the whole of the US – South, North, East, or West. Holographic also in that it has the coherent light of the laser, the homogeneity of the single elements scanned by the same beams. From the visual and plastic viewpoints too: things seem to be made of a more unreal substance; they seem to turn and move in a void as if by a special lighting effect, a fine membrane you pass through without noticing it. This is obviously true of the desert. It is also the case with Las Vegas and advertising, and even the activities of the people, public relations, and everyday electronics all stand out with the plasticity and simplicity of a beam of light. The hologram is akin to the world of phantasy. It is a three-dimensional dream and you can enter it as you would a dream. Everything depends on the existence of the ray of light bearing the objects. If it is interrupted, all the effects are dispersed, and reality along with it. You do indeed get the impression that America is made up of a fantastic switching between similar elements, and that everything is only held together by a thread of light, a laser beam, scanning out American reality before our eyes. In America the spectral does not refer to phantoms or to dancing ghosts, but to the spectrum into which light disperses.

On the aromatic hillsides of Santa Barbara, the villas are all like funeral homes. Between the gardenias and the eucalyptus trees, among the profusion of plant genuses and the monotony of the human species, lies the tragedy of a utopian dream made reality. In the very heartland of wealth and liberation, you always hear the same question: 'What are you doing after the orgy?' What do you do when everything is available – sex, flowers, the stereotypes of life and death? This is America's problem and, through America, it has become the whole world's problem.

All dwellings have something of the grave about them, but here the fake serenity is complete. The unspeakable house plants, lurking everywhere like the obsessive fear of death, the picture windows looking like Snow White's glass coffin, the clumps of pale, dwarf flowers stretched out in patches like sclerosis, the proliferation of technical gadgetry inside the house, beneath it, around it, like drips in an intensive care ward, the TV, stereo, and video which provide communication with the beyond, the car (or cars) that connect one up to that great shoppers' funeral parlour, the supermarket, and, lastly, the wife and children, as glowing symptoms of success . . . everything here testifies to death having found its ideal home.

The microwave, the waste disposal, the orgasmic elasticity of the carpets: this soft, resort-style civilization irresistibly evokes the end of the world. All their activities here have a surreptitious end-of-the-world feel to them: these Californian scholars with monomaniacal passions for things French or Marxist, the various sects obsessively concerned with chastity or crime, these joggers sleepwalking in the mist like shadows that have escaped from Plato's cave, the very real mental defectives or mongols let out of the psychiatric hospitals (this letting loose of the mad into the city seems a sure sign of the end of the world, the loosing of the seals of the Apocalypse), these obese individuals who have escaped from the hormone laboratories of their own bodies, and these drilling platforms – 'oil sanctuaries' – keeping watch in the night, like grand casinos, or extraterrestrial spacecraft.

Ravishing hyperrealism
Ecstatic asceticism
Multi-process tracking shot
Interactive multi-dimensionality
Mind-blowing

Western Digitals
Body Building Incorporated
Mileage Unlimited
Channel Zero

Seedy bar in Santa Barbara. The billiard player's red braces. Foucault, Sartre, and Orson Welles all standing together at the counter, talking to each other, strangely convincing, strikingly like the originals. 'Cocktail scenery.' The smell of violence, the stale odour of beer. 'Hustling is prohibited.'

Sex, beach, and mountains. Sex and beach, beach and mountains. Mountains and sex. A few concepts. Sex and concepts. 'Just a life.'

Everything is destined to reappear as simulation. Landscapes as photography, women as the sexual scenario, thoughts as writing, terrorism as fashion and the media, events as television. Things seem only to exist by virtue of this strange destiny. You wonder whether the world itself isn't just here to serve as advertising copy in some other world.

When the only physical beauty is created by plastic surgery, the only urban beauty by landscape surgery, the only opinion by opinion poll surgery . . . and now, with genetic engineering, along comes plastic surgery for the whole human species.

This is a culture which sets up specialized institutes so that people's bodies can come together and touch, and, at the same time, invents pans in which the water *does not touch* the bottom of the pan, which is made of a substance so homogeneous, dry, and artificial that not a single drop sticks to it, just like those bodies intertwined in 'feeling' and therapeutic love, which do not touch – not even for a moment. This is called interface or interaction. It has replaced face-to-face contact and action. It is also called communication, because these things really do communicate: the miracle is that the pan bottom communicates its heat to the water without touching it, in a sort of remote boiling process, in the same way as one body communicates its fluid, its erotic potential, to another without that other ever being seduced or even disturbed, by a sort of molecular capillary action. The code of separation has worked so well that they have even managed to separate the water from the pan and to make the pan transmit its heat *as a message*, or to make one body transmit its desire to the other as a message, as a fluid to be decoded. This is called information and it has wormed its way into everything, like a phobic, maniacal leitmotiv, which affects sexual relations as well as kitchen implements.

Other examples of this mania for asepsis:

The Getty museum where old paintings look new, bleached and gleaming, cleansed of all patina and *craquelure*, with an artificial lustre that echoes the fake Pompeian décor all around them.

In Philadelphia, a radical sect named 'MOVE', with a bizarre set of rules, including one forbidding both the practice of autopsy and the removal of rubbish, is cleared out by the police, who kill eleven people by fire and burn down thirty adjacent houses, including those (the irony of it!) of all the neighbours who had called for the sect to be removed.

This, too, is a clean-up operation. They are getting rid of rubbish and patina, getting back to an original state of cleanliness, restoring. 'Keep America clean.' And that smile everyone gives you as they pass, that friendly contraction of the jaws triggered by human warmth. It is the eternal smile of communication, the smile through which the child becomes aware of the presence of others, or struggles desperately with the problem of their presence. It is the equivalent of the primal scream of man alone in the world. Whether I am right in all this or not, they certainly do smile at you here, though neither from courtesy, nor from an effort to charm. This smile signifies only the need to smile. It is a bit like the Cheshire Cat's grin: it continues to float on faces long after all emotion has disappeared. A smile available at any moment, but half-scared to exist, to give itself away. No ulterior motive lurks behind it, but it keeps you at a distance. It is part of the general cryogenization of emotions. It is, indeed, the smile the dead man will wear in his funeral home, as he clings to a hope of maintaining contact even in the next world. The smile of immunity, the smile of advertising: 'This country is good. I am good. We are the best'. It is also Reagan's smile – the culmination of the self-satisfaction of the entire American nation – which is on the way to becoming the sole principle of government. An autoprophetic smile, like all signs in advertising. Smile and others will smile back. Smile to show how transparent, how candid you are. Smile if you have nothing to say. Most of all, do not hide the fact you have nothing to say nor your total indifference to others. Let this emptiness, this profound indifference shine out spontaneously in your smile. *Give* your emptiness and indifference to others, light up your face with the zero degree of joy and pleasure, smile, smile, smile . . . Americans may have no identity, but they do have wonderful teeth.

And it works. With this smile Reagan obtains a much wider consensus than any that could be achieved by a Kennedy with mere reason or political intelligence. The recourse to a pure form of compliment, be it animal or infantile, is much more successful and the whole American population comes together in this toothpaste effect. No idea – not even the nation's moral values in their entirety – could ever have produced such a result. Reagan's credibility is exactly equal to his transparency and the nullity of his smile.

The skateboarder with his Walkman, the intellectual working on his word-processor, the Bronx breakdancer whirling frantically in the Roxy, the jogger and the body-builder: everywhere, whether in regard to the body or the mental faculties, you find the same blank solitude, the same narcissistic refraction.

This omnipresent cult of the body is extraordinary. It is the only object on which everyone is made to concentrate, not as a source of pleasure, but as an object of frantic concern, in the obsessive fear of failure or substandard performance, a sign and an anticipation of death, that death to which no one can any longer give a meaning, but which everyone knows has at all times to be prevented. The body is cherished in the perverse certainty of its uselessness, in the total certainty of its non-resurrection. Now, pleasure is an effect of the resurrection of the body, by which it exceeds that hormonal, vascular and dietetic equilibrium in which we seek to imprison it, that exorcism by fitness and hygiene. So the body has to be made to forget pleasure as present grace, to forget its possible metamorphosis into other forms of appearance and become dedicated to the utopian preservation of a youth that is, in any case, already lost. For the body which doubts its own existence is already half-dead, and the current semi-yogic, semi-ecstatic cult of the body is a morbid preoccupation. The care taken of the body while it is alive prefigures the way it will be made up in the funeral home, where it will be given a smile that is really 'into' death.

This 'into' is the key to everything. The point is not to be nor even to *have* a body, but to be into your own body. Into your sexuality, into your own desire. Into your own functions, as if they were energy differentials or video screens. The hedonism of the 'into': the body is a scenario and the curious hygienist threnody devoted to it runs through the innumerable fitness centres, body-building gyms, stimulation and simulation studios that stretch from Venice to Tupanga Canyon, bearing witness to a collective asexual obsession.

This is echoed by the other obsession: that of being 'into', hooked in to your own brain. What people are contemplating on their word-processor screens is the operation of their own brains. It is not entrails that we try to interpret these days, nor even hearts or facial expressions; it is, quite simply, the brain. We want to expose to view its billions of connections and watch it operating like a video-game. All this cerebral, electronic snobbery is hugely affected – far from being the sign of a superior knowledge of humanity, it is merely the mark of a simplified theory, since the human being is here reduced to the terminal excrescence of his or her spinal cord. But we should not worry too much about this: it is all much less scientific, less functional than is ordinarily thought. All that fascinates us is the *spectacle* of the brain and its workings. What we are wanting here is to see our thoughts unfolding before us – and this itself is a superstition.

Hence, the academic grappling with his computer, ceaselessly correcting, reworking, and complexifying, turning the exercise into a kind of interminable psychoanalysis, memorizing everything in an effort to escape the final outcome, to delay the day of reckoning of death, and that other – fatal – moment of reckoning that is writing, by forming an endless feed-back loop with the machine. This is a marvellous instrument of exoteric magic. In fact all these interactions come down in the end to endless exchanges with a machine. Just look at the child sitting in front of his computer at school; do you think he has been made interactive, opened up to the world? Child and machine have merely been joined together in an integrated circuit. As for the intellectual, he has at last found the equivalent of what the teenager gets from his stereo and his Walkman: a spectacular desublimation of thought, his concepts as images on a screen.

In the Roxy, the sound-proofed bar dominates the dancefloor the way the screens dominate an air traffic control room or the technicians' gallery towers over a television studio. The club is a fluorescent milieu with spotlighting, strobe effects, dancers swept by beams of light . . . all of these the effects you find on screens. *And everyone is aware of this.* Today, no staging of bodies, no performance can be without its control screen. This is not there to see or reflect those taking part, with the distance and magic of the mirror. No, it is there as an instantaneous, depthless refraction. Video, everywhere, serves only this end: it is a screen of ecstatic refraction. As such, it has nothing of the traditional image or scene, or of traditional theatricality, and its purpose is not to present action or allow self-contemplation; its goal is *to be hooked up to itself.* Without this circular hook-up, without this brief, instantaneous network that a brain, an object, an event, or a discourse create by being hooked up to themselves, without this perpetual video, nothing has any meaning today. The mirror phase has given way to the video phase.

This is not narcissism and it is wrong to abuse that term to describe the effect. What develops around the video or stereo culture is not a narcissistic imaginary, but an effect of frantic self-referentiality, a short-circuit which immediately hooks up like with like, and, in so doing, emphasizes their surface intensity and deeper meaninglessness.

This is the special effect of our times. The ecstasy of the Polaroid is of the same order: to hold the object and its image almost simultaneously as if the conception of light of ancient physics or metaphysics, in which each object was thought to secrete doubles or negatives of itself that we pick up with our eyes, has become a reality. It is a dream. It is the optical materialization of a magical process. The Polaroid photo is a sort of ecstatic membrane that has come away from the real object.

You stop a horse that is bolting. You do not stop a jogger who is jogging. Foaming at the mouth, his mind riveted on the inner countdown to the moment when he will achieve a higher plane of consciousness, he is not to be stopped. If you stopped him to ask the time, he would bite your head off. He doesn't have a bit between his teeth, though he may perhaps be carrying dumb-bells or even weights in his belt (where are the days when girls used to wear bracelets on their ankles?). What the third-century Stylite sought in self-privation and proud stillness, he is seeking through the muscular exhaustion of his body. He is the brother in mortification of those who conscientiously exhaust themselves in the body-building studios on complicated machines with chrome pulleys and on terrifying medical contraptions. There is a direct line that runs from the medieval instruments of torture, via the industrial movements of production-line work, to the techniques of schooling the body by using mechanical apparatuses. Like dieting, body-building, and so many other things, jogging is a new form of voluntary servitude (it is also a new form of adultery).

*   *   *

Decidedly, joggers are the true Latter Day Saints and the protagonists of an easy-does-it Apocalypse. Nothing evokes the end of the world more than a man running straight ahead on a beach, swathed in the sounds of his Walkman, cocooned in the solitary sacrifice of his energy, indifferent even to catastrophes since he expects destruction to come only as the fruit of his own efforts, from exhausting the energy of a body that has in his own eyes become useless. Primitives, when in despair, would commit suicide by swimming out to sea until they could swim no longer. The jogger commits suicide by running up and down the beach. His eyes are wild, saliva drips from his mouth. Do not stop him. He will either hit you or simply carry on dancing around in front of you like a man possessed.

The only comparable distress is that of a man eating alone in the heart of the city. You see people doing that in New York, the human flotsam of conviviality, no longer even concealing themselves to eat leftovers in public. But this still belongs to the world of urban, industrial poverty. The thousands of lone men, each running on their own account, with no thought for others, with a stereophonic fluid in their heads that oozes through into their eyes, that is the world of *Blade Runner*, the post-catastrophe world. Not to be aware of the natural light of California, nor even of a mountain fire that has been driven ten miles out to sea by the hot wind, and is enveloping the offshore oil platforms in its smoke, to see nothing of all this and obstinately to carry on running by a sort of lymphatic flagellation till sacrificial exhaustion is reached, that is truly a sign from the beyond. It is like the obese person who keeps on getting fatter, the record rotating endlessly in the same groove, the cells of a tumour proliferating, like everything that has lost the formula for stopping itself. This entire society, including its active, productive part – everyone – is running straight ahead, because they have lost the formula for stopping.

All these track-suits and jogging suits, these loose-fitting shorts and baggy cotton shirts, these 'easy clothes' are actually old bits of nightwear, and all these relaxed walkers and runners have not yet left the night behind. As a result of wearing these billowing clothes, their bodies have come to float in their clothes and they themselves float in their own bodies.

Anorexic culture: a culture of disgust, of expulsion, of anthropoemia, of rejection. Characteristic of a period of obesity, saturation, overabundance.

The anorexic prefigures this culture in rather a poetic fashion by trying to keep it at bay. He refuses lack. He says: I lack nothing, therefore I shall not eat. With the overweight person, it is the opposite: he refuses fullness, repletion. He says: I lack everything, so I will eat anything at all. The anorexic staves off lack by emptiness, the overweight person staves off fullness by excess. Both are homeopathic final solutions, solutions by extermination.

The jogger has yet another solution. In a sense, he spews himself out; he doesn't merely expend his energy in his running, he vomits it. He has to attain the ecstasy of fatigue, the 'high' of mechanical annihilation, just as the anorexic aims for the 'high' of organic annihilation, the ecstasy of the empty body and the obese individual seeks the high of dimensional annihilation: the ecstasy of the full body.

The latest obsession of American public opinion: the sexual abuse of children. There is now a law that two people must be present when very young children are being handled for fear of unverifiable sexual abuse. At the same time, supermarket carrier bags are adorned with the portraits of missing children.

Protect everything, detect everything, contain everything – obsessional society.

Save time. Save energy. Save money. Save our souls – phobic society.

Low tar. Low energy. Low calories. Low sex. Low speed – anorexic society.

Curiously, in this world where everything is available in profusion, everything has to be saved and economized. The obsession of a young society, concerned to protect its future? The impression given is rather that of a sense of threat, all the more insidious for being groundless. It is profusion which creates an hallucination of a sort of backfiring into shortage and penury, which has to be averted by homeopathic discipline. There are no other reasons for these starvation rations – collective dieting, ecological control, this mortification of bodies and pleasures. A whole society organized to ward off the vengeance of overfed divinities, suffocated by plenty. Of course our basic problem today is how to avoid becoming overweight.

Compiling inventories of everything, stocking everything, memorizing everything.

Hence the elephants enveloped in liquid bitumen, whose bones become fossilized in its black, mineral viscosity, together with the lions, mammoths, and wolves who roamed the plains of Los Angeles and were the first, prehistoric victims of the oil fields. Today they have all received a second embalming at Hancock Park in a museum devoted to the rote-learning of prehistory. And, in conformity with the prevailing moral code, all this is presented with conviction. Americans are people *of conviction*, convinced of everything and seeking to convince. One of the aspects of their good faith is this stubborn determination to reconstitute everything of a past and a history which were not their own and which they have largely destroyed or spirited away. Renaissance castles, fossilized elephants, Indians on reservations, sequoias as holograms, etc.

In storing details on their computers of all the known souls in the civilized (white) countries, the Mormons of Salt Lake City are behaving no differently from other Americans, who all share the same missionary spirit. It is never too late to revive your origins. It is their destiny: since they were not the first to be in on history, they will be the first to immortalize everything by reconstitution (by putting things in museums, they can match in an instant the fossilization process nature took millions of years to complete). But the conception Americans have of the museum is much wider than our own. To them, everything is worthy of protection, embalming, restoration. Everything can have a second birth, the eternal birth of the simulacrum. Not only are the Americans missionaries, they are also Anabaptists: having missed out on the original baptism, they dream of baptizing everything a second time and only accord value to this later sacrament which is, as we know, a repeat performance of the first, but its repetition *as something more real*. And this indeed is the perfect definition of the simulacrum. All Anabaptists are sectarian, and sometimes violent. Americans are no exception to this rule. To reconstruct things in their exact form, so as to present them on the Day of Judgement, they are prepared to destroy and exterminate – Thomas Müntzer was an Anabaptist.

It is not by chance that it is the Mormons who run the world's biggest computerization project: the recording of twenty generations of living souls throughout the world, a process which is seen as a rebaptizing of those souls, bringing them a new promise of salvation. Evangelization has become a mission of mutants, of extraterrestrials, and if it has progressed (?) in that direction, it is thanks to the latest memory-storage techniques. And these have been made possible by the deep puritanism of computer science, an intensely Calvinistic, Presbyterian discipline, which has inherited the universal and scientific rigidity of the techniques for achieving salvation by good works. The Counter-Reformation methods of the Catholic Church, with its naive sacramental practices, its cults, its more archaic and popular beliefs, could never compete with this modernity.

Executive Terminal
Basic Extermination
Metastatic Consumption

Everywhere survival has become a burning issue, perhaps by some obscure weariness of life or a collective desire for catastrophe (though we should not take all this too seriously: it is also a playing at catastrophe). Certainly, this whole panoply of survival issues – dieting, ecology, saving the sequoias, seals or the human race – tends to prove that we are very much alive (just as all imaginary fairy-tales tend to prove that the real world is very real). But this is not so certain, for not only is the fact of living not really well-attested, but the paradox of this society is that you cannot even die in it any more since you are already dead . . . This is real suspense. And it is not simply an effect of living in the nuclear age, but derives from the ease with which we now live, which makes survivors of us all. If the bomb drops, we shall neither have the time to die nor any awareness of dying. But already in our hyper-protected society we no longer have any awareness of death, since we have subtly passed over into a state where life is excessively easy.

The holocaust created an anticipatory form of such a condition. What the inmates of the concentration camps were deprived of was the very possibility of having control of their own deaths, of playing, even gambling with their own deaths, making their deaths a sacrifice: they were robbed of power over their own deaths. And this is what is happening to all of us, in slow, homeopathic doses, by virtue of the very development of our systems. The explosions and the extermination (Auschwitz and Hiroshima) still go on, though they have simply taken on a purulent, endemic form. The chain reaction continues nonetheless, the contagion, the unfolding of the viral and bacteriological process. The end of history was precisely the inauguration of this chain reaction.

The obsessive desire for survival (and not for *life*) is a symptom of this state of affairs and doubtless also the most worrying sign of the degradation of the species. If you think about the forms that desire currently takes – antinuclear shelters, cryogenization, high-pressure therapy – you see that they are exactly the forms of extermination. To avoid dying, one chooses to withdraw into some protective bubble or other. In this light, we should take it as a reassuring sign that people lost interest in antinuclear protection so quickly (the shelter market has become a mere prestige market, like the market for artworks or luxury yachts). It seems that people have become tired of nuclear blackmail and decided not to give in to it, leaving the threat of destruction hanging in mid-air over them, perhaps with an obscure sense of how unreal it is. A fine example of a vital reaction disguised as resignation. 'If we have to die, better to die in the open air than in an underground sarcophagus.' At a stroke an end is put to survival blackmail and life can go on.

Everyone is weary of these apocalyptic visions – the great scenario of the nuclear threat, the theatrical negotiations, 'Star Wars'. In the end, they defend themselves with a lack of imagination. Even attempts to stimulate that imagination in films like *The Last Day* have not worked. Nothing has ever been able to make this nuclear scene – or obscenity – credible. With delicate matters like this (as with cancer), imagining death has the effect of bringing the fatal event closer. The masses' silent indifference to nuclear pathos (whether it comes from the nuclear powers or from antinuclear campaigners) is therefore a great sign of hope and a political fact of the utmost importance.

There is a science–fiction story in which a number of very rich people wake up one morning in their luxury villas in the mountains to find that they are encircled by a transparent and insuperable obstacle, a wall of glass that has appeared in the night. From the depths of their vitrified luxury, they can still just discern the outside world, the real universe from which they are cut off, which has suddenly become the ideal world. But it is too late. These rich people will die slowly in their aquarium like goldfish. Some of the university campuses here remind me of this.

Lost among the pine trees, the fields, and the rivers (it is an old ranch that was donated to the university), and made up of little blocks, each one out of sight of the others, like the people who live in them: this one is Santa Cruz. It's a bit like the Bermuda Triangle (or Santa Barbara). Everything vanishes. Everything gets sucked in. Total decentring, total community. After the ideal city of the future, the ideal cosy nook. Nothing converges on a single point, neither the traffic, nor the architecture, nor authority. But, by that very token, it also becomes impossible to hold a demonstration: where could you assemble? Demonstrations can only go round and round in the forest, where the participants alone can see them. Of all the Californian campuses, famous for their spaciousness and charm, this is the most idealized, the most naturalized. It is the epitome of all that is beautiful. Famous architects designed the buildings and the bays of Carmel and Monterey stretch out all around. If the conviviality of the future already exists somewhere, then this must be the place. And yet this freedom, protected both by the pleasantness of the vegetation and by academic openness, becomes its own prisoner once again, immured in a natural and social over-protectedness which ends up producing all the agonies of the carceral universe (precisely by virtue of its walls, the carceral system may in certain conditions evolve in the direction of utopia more rapidly than open social systems). Society has become emancipated here as nowhere else on earth. The psychiatric hospitals have been opened up, public transport is free, and yet paradoxically this ideal has become closed in on itself as if behind a wall of glass.

A paradisiac and inward-looking illusion. We might understand what Lyotard calls the 'Pacific Wall' as the wall of crystal that imprisons California in its own beatitude. But whereas the demand for happiness used to be something oceanic and emancipatory, here it comes wrapped up in a foetal tranquillity. Are there still passions, murders, and acts of violence in this strange, padded, wooded, pacified, convivial republic? Yes, but the violence is autistic and reactional. There are no crimes of passion, but there are rapes, and a case where a dozen women were murdered in two years before the killer was discovered. This is foetal violence, as gratuitous as 'automatic writing'. It seems an expression not so much of real aggression as of nostalgia for the old prohibitions (why does the number of rapes increase with the degree of sexual liberation?).

How sentimental these mixed dormitories seem, opening out here on to the forest, as if nature itself could be convivial and maternal, could herself stand as guarantor for the blossoming of sexuality and the ecology of manners, as if nature could look sympathetically upon any human society, as if one could have some relationship with her, outside the cruel universe of magic, which was not *stoical*, not the Stoics' relation between a blind, pitiless necessity and the even greater defiance, the even greater freedom one has to counterpose to it. Here, every last vestige of a heroic sense of destiny has disappeared. The whole place exudes an air of sentimental reconciliation with nature, with sex, with madness and even with history (by way of a carefully corrected, revised Marxism).

Like many other aspects of contemporary America, Santa Cruz is part of *the post-orgy world*, the world left behind after the great social and sexual convulsions. The refugees from the orgy – the orgy of sex, political violence, the Vietnam War, the Woodstock Crusade, and the ethnic and anti-capitalist struggles too, together with the passion for money, the passion for success, hard technologies etc., in short, the whole orgy of modernity – are all there, jogging along in their tribalism, which is akin to the electronic tribalism of Silicon Valley. Reduced pace of work, decentralization, air-conditioning, soft technologies. Paradise. But a very slight modification, a change of just a few degrees, would suffice to make it seem like hell.

A new development in the field of sexuality. The orgy is over, liberation is over; it is not sex one is looking for but one's 'gender', i.e. both one's 'look' and its genetic formula. People no longer oscillate between desire and its fulfilment, but between their genetic formula and their sexual identity (to be discovered). This is a new erotic culture. After a culture based on prohibition ('What are your prerequisites for sex?' – 'The door has to be locked, the lights have to be out, and my mother has to be in another State'), this is a culture based on the questioning of one's own definition: 'Am I sexed? What sex am I? Ultimately, is sex necessary? What does sexual difference consist in?' Liberation has left everyone in an undefined state (it is always the same: once you are liberated, you are forced to ask who you are). After a triumphalist phase, the assertion of female sexuality has become as fragile as that of male sexuality. No one knows where they are. This is why there's so much love-making, so many children produced: there at least you still have proof that two people are needed *so difference still exists*. But not for long. Already, the 'muscle-woman', who, simply by using her vaginal muscles, manages to reproduce the effect of male penetration exactly, is a good example of self-referentiality and of getting along without difference – she at least has found her label.

The more general problem is one of an absence of difference, bound up with a decline in the display of sexual characteristics. The outer signs of masculinity are tending towards zero, but so are the signs of femininity. It is in this conjuncture that we have seen new idols emerging, idols who take up the challenge of undefinedness and who play at mixing genres/genders. 'Gender benders'. Neither masculine nor feminine, but not homosexual either. Boy George, Michael Jackson, David Bowie . . . Whereas the idols of the previous generation were explosive figures of sex and pleasure, these new idols pose for everyone the question of the *play* of difference and their own lack of definition. They are exceptional figures. For want of an identity, most of them have gone in search of a 'gender model', a generic formula. Some kind of differentiating feature has to be found, so why not look for it in fashion . . . or in genetics? A 'look' based on clothes, or a 'look' based on cells. Any old gimmick will do, any idiom. The question of difference is more crucial than that of pleasure. Are we seeing here a post-modern version of a sexual liberation that is now past and gone, that liberation as mere fashion, or is this a bio-sociological mutation in our own self-perception, based upon the sexual losing the priority it formerly enjoyed, a priority which characterized the whole modern period? 'Gender Research: a New Frontier?'

Pushed to its logical conclusions, this would leave neither masculine nor feminine, but a dissemination of individual sexes referring only to themselves, each one managed as an independent enterprise. The end of seduction, the end of difference, and a slide towards a different system of values. An astonishing paradox emerges: sexuality might become once again a merely secondary problem, as it was in most earlier societies, and be eclipsed by other stronger symbolic systems (birth, hierarchy, asceticism, glory, death). This would prove that sexuality was after all only one possible model among many, and not the most crucial. But what might those new models be today (for in the meantime all the others have disappeared)? The model that seems likely to emerge is that of an ideal of performance, of the genetic fulfilment of one's own formula. In business, in emotional life, in their projects and their pleasures, everyone will seek to develop their optimum programme. Everyone will have their code, their formula. But also their 'look', their image. So shall we perhaps get something like a genetic 'look'?

Irvine: a new Silicon Valley. Electronic factories with no openings to the outside world, like integrated circuits. A desert zone, given over to ions and electrons, a supra-human place, the product of inhuman decision-making. By a terrible twist of irony it just had to be here, in the hills of Irvine, that they shot *Planet of the Apes*. But, on the lawn, the American squirrels tell us all is well, and that America is kind to animals, to itself, and to the rest of the world, and that in everyone's heart there is a slumbering squirrel. The whole Walt Disney philosophy eats out of your hand with these pretty little sentimental creatures in grey fur coats. For my own part, I believe that behind these smiling eyes there lurks a cold, ferocious beast fearfully stalking us . . . On the same lawn with the squirrels stands a sign put there by some society or other of Jesus: 'Vietnam, Cambodia, Lebanon, Grenada – We are a violent society in a violent world!'

There is nothing funny about Halloween. This sarcastic festival reflects, rather, an infernal demand for revenge by children on the adult world. The threat from this evil force hangs over adults here, equal in intensity only to their devotion to children. There is nothing more unhealthy than this childish sorcery, behind all the dressing up and the presents – people turn out their lights and hide, for fear of harassment. And it is no accident that some of them stick needles or razor blades into the apples or cookies they hand out to the children.

Laughter on American television has taken the place of the chorus in Greek tragedy. It is unrelenting; the news, the stock-exchange reports, and the weather forecast are about the only things spared. But so obsessive is it that you go on hearing it behind the voice of Reagan or the Marines disaster in Beirut. Even behind the adverts. It is the monster from *Alien* prowling around in all the corridors of the spaceship. It is the sarcastic exhilaration of a puritan culture. In other countries, the business of laughing is left to the viewers. Here, their laughter is put on the screen, integrated into the show. It is the screen that is laughing and having a good time. You are simply left alone with your consternation.

Vietnam on television (a pleonasm, since it always was a television war). The Americans fight with two essential weapons: air power and information. That is, with the physical bombardment of the enemy and the electronic bombardment of the rest of the world. These are non-territorial weapons, whilst all the Vietnamese weapons and all their tactics were products of the people and its territory.

That is why the war was won by both sides: by the Vietnamese on the ground, by the Americans in the electronic mental space. And if the one side won an ideological and political victory, the other made *Apocalypse Now* and that has gone right around the world.

The obsessive fear of the Americans is that the lights might go out. Lights are left on all night in the houses. In the tower blocks the empty offices remain lit. On the freeways, in broad daylight, the cars keep all their headlights on. In Palms Ave., Venice, California, a little grocery store that sells beer in a part of town where no one is on the streets after 7 p.m. leaves its orange and green neon sign flashing all night, into the void. And this is not to mention the television, with its twenty-four-hour schedules, often to be seen functioning like an hallucination in the empty rooms of houses or vacant hotel rooms – as in the Porterville hotel where the curtains were torn, the water cut off, and the doors swinging in the wind, but on the fluorescent screen in each of the rooms a TV commentator was describing the take-off of the space shuttle. There is nothing more mysterious than a TV set left on in an empty room. It is even stranger than a man talking to himself or a woman standing dreaming at her stove. It is as if another planet is communicating with you. Suddenly the TV reveals itself for what it really is: a video of another world, ultimately addressed to no one at all, delivering its images indifferently, indifferent to its own messages (you can easily imagine it still functioning after humanity has disappeared). In short, in America the arrival of night-time or periods of rest cannot be accepted, nor can the Americans bear to see the technological process halted. Everything has to be working all the time, there has to be no let-up in man's artificial power, and the intermittent character of natural cycles (the seasons, day and night, heat and cold) has to be replaced by a functional continuum that is sometimes absurd (deep down, there is the same refusal of the intermittent nature of true and false: everything is true; and of good and evil: everything is good). You may seek to explain this in terms of fear, perhaps obsessional fear, or say that this unproductive expenditure is an act of mourning. But what is absurd is also admirable. The skylines lit up at dead of night, the air-conditioning systems cooling empty hotels in the desert and artificial light in the middle of the day all have something both demented and admirable about them. The mindless luxury of a rich civilization, and yet of a civilization perhaps as scared to see the lights go out as was the hunter in his primitive night. There is some truth in all of this. But what is striking is the fascination with artifice, with energy and space. And not only natural space: space is spacious in their heads as well.

All great world powers have at some time or another created their monumental avenues which provided, as one looked down them, a miniature representation of the infinitude of empire. But the Aztecs at Teotihuacan, the Egyptians in the Valley of Kings, and Louis XIV at Versailles all created these syntheses in an architecture that was their own. Here in Washington, the vast panorama that stretches from the Lincoln Memorial to the Capitol is made up of a series of museums encapsulating our entire universe from Stone Age to Space Age. This gives the whole thing a science-fiction feel, as if an attempt had been made to gather all the marks of earthly endeavour and culture together here for the benefit of a visitor from outer space. And the White House, standing just alongside, watching discreetly over the whole, itself comes to look like a museum, the museum of world power, with an air of remoteness and prophylactic whiteness.

There is nothing to match flying over Los Angeles by night. A sort of luminous, geometric, incandescent immensity, stretching as far as the eye can see, bursting out from the cracks in the clouds. Only Hieronymus Bosch's hell can match this inferno effect. The muted fluorescence of all the diagonals: Wilshire, Lincoln, Sunset, Santa Monica. Already, flying over San Fernando Valley, you come upon the horizontal infinite in every direction. But, once you are beyond the mountain, a city ten times larger hits you. You will never have encountered anything that stretches as far as this before. Even the sea cannot match it, since it is not divided up geometrically. The irregular, scattered flickering of European cities does not produce the same parallel lines, the same vanishing points, the same aerial perspectives either. They are medieval cities. This one condenses by night the entire future geometry of the networks of human relations, gleaming in their abstraction, luminous in their extension, astral in their reproduction to infinity. Mulholland Drive by night is an extraterrestrial's vantage-point on earth, or conversely, an earth-dweller's vantage-point on the Galactic metropolis.

Dawn in Los Angeles, coming up over the Hollywood hills. You get the distinct feeling that the sun only touched Europe lightly on its way to rising properly here, above this plane geometry where its light is still that brand new light of the edge of the desert. Long-stemmed palm trees, swaying in front of the electronic billboard, the only vertical signs in this two-dimensional world.

At 6 a.m. a man is already telephoning from a public phonebox in Beverly Terrace. The neon signs of the night are going out as the daytime ones become visible. The light everywhere reveals and illuminates the absence of architecture. This is what gives the city its beauty, this city that is so intimate and warm, whatever anyone says of it: the fact is it is in love with its limitless horizontality, as New York may be with its verticality.

Los Angeles Freeways

Gigantic, spontaneous spectacle of automotive traffic. A total collective act, staged by the entire population, twenty-four hours a day. By virtue of the sheer size of the layout and the kind of complicity that binds this network of thoroughfares together, traffic rises here to the level of a dramatic attraction, acquires the status of symbolic organization. The machines themselves, with their fluidity and their automatic transmission, have created a milieu in their own image, a milieu into which you insert yourself gently, which you switch over to as you might switch over to a TV channel. Unlike our European motorways, which are unique, directional axes, and are therefore still places of expulsion (Virilio), the freeway system is a place of integration (they even say that there are families who drive round on these roads in their mobile homes without ever leaving). It creates a different state of mind, and the European driver very quickly gives up his aggressive, every-man-for-himself behaviour and his individual reactions, and adopts the rules of this collective game. There is something of the freedom of movement that you have in the desert here, and indeed Los Angeles, with its extensive structure, is merely an inhabited fragment of the desert. Thus the freeways do not de-nature the city or the landscape; they simply pass through it and unravel it without altering the desert character of this particular metropolis. And they are ideally suited to the only truly profound pleasure, that of keeping on the move.

To the person who knows the American freeways, their signs read like a litany. 'Right lane must exit.' This 'must exit' has always struck me as a sign of destiny. I have got to go, to expel myself from this paradise, leave this providential highway which leads nowhere, but keeps me in touch with everyone. This is the only real society or warmth here, this collective propulsion, this compulsion – a compulsion of lemmings plunging suicidally together. Why should I tear myself away to revert to an individual trajectory, a vain sense of responsibility? 'Must exit': you are being sentenced. You are a player being exiled from the only – useless and glorious – form of collective existence. 'Through traffic merge left': they tell you everything, everything is announced. Merely reading the signs that are essential to your survival gives you an extraordinary feeling of instant lucidity, of reflex 'participation', immediate and smooth. Of a functional participation that is reflected in certain precise gestures. The lines of traffic diverging towards Ventura Freeway and San Diego Freeway do not leave one another, they just separate out. At every hour of the day approximately the same number split off towards Hollywood or towards Santa Monica. Pure, statistical energy, a ritual being acted out – the regularity of the flows cancels out individual destinations. What you have here is the charm of ceremonies: you have the whole of space before you, just as ceremonies have the whole of time before them.

The point is not to write the sociology or psychology of the car, the point is to drive. That way you learn more about this society than all academia could ever tell you.

The way American cars have of leaping into action, of taking off so smoothly, by virtue of their automatic transmission and power steering. Pulling away effortlessly, noiselessly eating up the road, gliding along without the slightest bump (the surfaces of the highways and freeways are remarkable, matched only by the fluidity of the cars' performance), braking smoothly but instantly, riding along as if you were on a cushion of air, leaving behind the old obsession with what is coming up ahead, or what is overtaking you (there is an unspoken agreement on collective driving here; in Europe we have only the highway code). All this creates a new experience of space, and, at the same time, a new experience of the whole social system. All you need to know about American society can be gleaned from an anthropology of its driving behaviour. That behaviour tells you much more than you could ever learn from its political ideas. Drive ten thousand miles across America and you will know more about the country than all the institutes of sociology and political science put together.

The city was here before the freeway system, no doubt, but it now looks as though the metropolis has actually been built around this arterial network. It is the same with American reality. It was there before the screen was invented, but everything about the way it is today suggests it was invented with the screen in mind, that it is the refraction of a giant screen. This is not like a Platonic shadowplay, but more as if everything were carried along by, and haloed in, the gleam of the screen. Along with flux and mobility, the screen and its refraction are fundamental determinants of everyday events. A fusion of the kinetic and the cinematic produces a different mental configuration and overall perception from our own. You do not find mobility or the screen taking precedence over reality in the same way in Europe, where things most often remain within the static form of territory, the palpable form of substances.

*   *   *

In fact, the cinema here is not where you think it is. It is certainly not to be found in the studios the tourist crowds flock to – Universal, Paramount, etc., those subdivisions of Disneyland. If you believe that the whole of the Western world is hypostatized in America, the whole of America in California, and California in MGM and Disneyland, then this is the microcosm of the West.

In fact what you are presented with in the studios is the degeneration of the cinematographic illusion, its mockery, just as what is offered in Disneyland is a parody of the world of the imagination. The sumptuous age of stars and images is reduced to a few artificial tornado effects, pathetic fake buildings, and childish tricks which the crowd pretends to be taken in by to avoid feeling too disappointed. Ghost towns, ghost people. The whole place has the same air of obsolescence about it as Sunset or Hollywood Boulevard. You come out feeling as though you have been put through some infantile simulation test. Where is the cinema? It is all around you outside, all over the city, that marvellous, continuous performance of films and scenarios. Everywhere but here.

It is not the least of America's charms that even outside the movie theatres the whole country is cinematic. The desert you pass through is like the set of a Western, the city a screen of signs and formulas. It is the same feeling you get when you step out of an Italian or a Dutch gallery into a city that seems the very reflection of the paintings you have just seen, as if the city had come out of the paintings and not the other way about. The American city seems to have stepped right out of the movies. To grasp its secret, you should not, then, begin with the city and move inwards to the screen; you should begin with the screen and move outwards to the city. It is there that cinema does not assume an exceptional form, but simply invests the streets and the entire town with a mythical atmosphere. That is where it is truly gripping. This is why the cult of stars is not a secondary phenomenon, but the supreme form of cinema, its mythical transfiguration, the last great myth of our modernity. Precisely because the idol is merely a pure, contagious image, a violently realized ideal. They say that stars give you something to dream about, but there is a difference between dreaming and fascination by images. The screen idols are immanent in the unfolding of life as a series of images. They are a system of luxury prefabrication, brilliant syntheses of the stereotypes of life and love. *They embody one single passion only: the passion for images*, and the immanence of desire in the image. They are not something to dream about; they are the dream. And they have all the characteristics of dreams: they produce a marked condensation (crystallization) effect and an effect of contiguity (they are immediately contagious), and, above all, they have that power of instantaneous visual materialization (*Anschaulichkeit*) of desire, which is also a feature of dreams. They do not, therefore, feed the romantic or sexual imagination; they are immediate visibility, immediate transcription, material collage, precipitation of desire. Fetishes, fetish objects, that have nothing to do with the world of the imagination, but everything to do with *the material fiction of the image*.

In 1989 the Revolutionary Olympic Games will be held in Los Angeles to mark the bicentenary of the French Revolution. The flame of history passes to the West Coast. This is normal. Everything that disappears in Europe is born again in San Francisco. We may envisage a reconstruction of the great revolutionary scenes in giant holograms, the most extensive archives, a complete film library, the best actors, the best historians. A century from now you will not be able to tell the difference. It will be as if the Revolution had taken place here. If the Getty Villa at Malibu were suddenly engulfed by lava, what difference would there be, a few centuries from now, between that building and the ruins of Pompeii?

What would the promoters of the bicentenary do if a new revolution broke out between now and 1989? But there is no way that can happen. And yet you cannot help but wish that the actual event might really occur and short-circuit the simulacrum, or that the simulacrum might itself end in catastrophe. In the same way, at Universal Studios, you hope constantly that the special effects will turn into some real drama. But this is a final nostalgia which has actually been exploited by the cinema itself (*Westworld, Future World*). The Olympic Games – total happening, collective participation in national self-celebration. 'We did it!' We are the best. Reagan style. It would have taken another Leni Riefenstahl to film this new Berlin '36. Totally sponsored, totally euphoric, totally clean, a 100 per cent advertising event.

No accidents, no catastrophes, no terrorism, no traffic-jams on the freeways, no panic and . . . no Soviets. In short, an image of an ideal world, for the whole world to see. But after the national orgasm a sort of collective melancholy comes over the Angelinos, showing how provincial this metropolis still is.

If you get out of your car in this centrifugal metropolis, you immediately become a delinquent; as soon as you start walking, you are a threat to public order, like a dog wandering in the road. Only immigrants from the Third World are allowed to walk. It is, in a sense, their privilege, a privilege that goes along with that of occupying the empty hearts of the big cities. For other people, walking, fatigue, or muscular activity have become rare commodities, 'services' costing a lot of money. Thus, ironically, the old state of affairs has been inverted. Similarly, the queues at high-class restaurants or fashionable nightclubs are often longer than those at soup kitchens. This is democracy. The signs of the most utter poverty always have at least a chance of becoming fashionable.

One of America's specific problems is fame and glory, partly on account of its extreme rarity these days, but also because of its extreme vulgarization. 'In the future, everyone will be famous for fifteen minutes' (Andy Warhol). And it is true. Take, for example, the man who got on the wrong plane and found himself carted off to Auckland, New Zealand, instead of Oakland, near San Francisco. This event made him the hero of the day. He was interviewed everywhere and they are making a film about him. In this country, it is not the highest virtue, nor the heroic act, that achieves fame, but the uncommon nature of the least significant destiny. There is plenty for everyone, then, since the more conformist the system as a whole becomes, the more millions of individuals there are who are set apart by some tiny peculiarity. The slightest vibration in a statistical model, the tiniest whim of a computer are enough to bathe some piece of abnormal behaviour, however banal, in a fleeting glow of fame.

Like this white Christ carrying a heavy cross down Main Street, Venice. It is a very hot day. You want to tell him it has already been done, two thousand years ago. But he is not trying to do anything new. He is just carrying his cross the same way as other people carry 'Jesus Saves' or 'Know Jesus' badges on their cars. You could point out that no one – not a single person – is watching, and that he is accorded only indifference and derision as he passes. But he would tell you that was exactly how it was two thousand years ago.

The top of the Bonaventure Hotel. Its metal structure and its plate-glass windows rotate slowly around the cocktail bar. The movement of the skyscrapers outside is almost imperceptible. Then you realize that it is the platform of the bar that is moving, while the rest of the building remains still. In the end I get to see the whole city revolve around the top of the hotel. A dizzy feeling, which continues inside the hotel as a result of its labyrinthine convolution. Is this still architecture, this pure illusionism, this mere box of spatio-temporal tricks? Ludic and hallucinogenic, is this post-modern architecture?

No interior/exterior interface. The glass facades merely reflect the environment, sending back its own image. This makes them much more formidable than any wall of stone. It's just like people who wear dark glasses. Their eyes are hidden and others see only their own reflection. Everywhere the transparency of interfaces ends in internal refraction. Everything pretentiously termed 'communication' and 'interaction' – Walkman, dark glasses, automatic household appliances, hi-tech cars, even the perpetual dialogue with the computer – ends up with each monad retreating into the shade of its own formula, into its self-regulating little corner and its artificial immunity. Blocks like the Bonaventure building claim to be perfect, self-sufficient miniature cities. But they cut themselves off from the city more than they interact with it. They stop seeing it. They refract it like a dark surface. And you cannot get out of the building itself. You cannot fathom out its internal space, but it has no mystery; it is just like those games where you have to join all the dots together without any line crossing another. Here too everything connects, without any two pairs of eyes ever meeting.

It is the same outside.

A camouflaged individual, with a long beak, feathers, and a yellow cagoule, a madman in fancy dress, wanders along the sidewalks downtown, and nobody, but nobody, looks at him. They do not look at other people here. They are much too afraid they will throw themselves upon them with unbearable, sexual demands, requests for money or affection. Everything is charged with a somnambulic violence and you must avoid contact to escape its potential discharge. Now that the mad have been let out of the asylums everyone is seen as a potential madman. Everything is so informal, there is so little in the way of reserve or manners (except for that eternal film of a smile, which offers only a very flimsy protection), that you feel anything could blow up at any moment. By some chain reaction, all this latent hysteria could be released at a stroke. The same feeling in New York, where panic is almost the characteristic smell of the city streets. Sometimes it takes the form of a gigantic breakdown, as in 1976.

All around, the tinted glass facades of the buildings are like faces: frosted surfaces. It is as though there were no one inside the buildings, as if there were no one behind the faces. And there *really* is no one. This is what the ideal city is like.

First International Bank. Crocker Bank. Bank of America. Pentecostal Savings (or is that one a church?). All bunched together in the heart of the city, alongside the big airlines.

Money is fluid. Like grace, it is never yours. Coming to claim it is an offence against the divinity. Have you deserved this favour? Who are you and what are you going to do with it? You are suspected of wanting to put it to some use, and an evil one no doubt, whereas money is so beautiful in the fluid and intemporal state it is in at the bank, when it is being invested rather than spent. Shame on you and kiss the hand that gives it to you.

It is true that ownership of money burns your fingers, like power. We need people to take this risk for us and we should be eternally grateful to them. This is why I hesitate to deposit money in a bank. I am afraid I shall never dare to take it out again. When you go to confession and entrust your sins to the safe-keeping of the priest, do you ever come back for them? And yet the atmosphere in a bank is that of the confessional (there is no more Kafkaesque situation): admit that you have money, confess that this is not normal. And it is true: having money is an awkward situation, from which the bank is only too happy to deliver you: 'Your money interests us' – the bank holds you to ransom, its greed knows no bounds. Its immodest gaze reveals your private parts to you, and you are forced to hand your money over to appease it. One day I tried to close my account, taking all the money out in cash. The teller would not let me go with such a sum on me: it was obscene, dangerous, immoral. Would I not at least take travellers' cheques? 'No, the whole lot in cash'. I was mad. In America, you are stark raving mad if, instead of believing in money and its marvellous fluidity, you want to carry it round on you in banknotes. Money is dirty; that you must admit. And we really do need all these concrete and metal sanctuaries to protect us from it. So banks fulfil a crucial social function, and it is quite logical that these buildings should form the monumental heart of every town and city.

One of the finest things there is, at dawn: the Santa Monica Pier, with the white waves rolling in, the sky grey over Venice, the pale green or turquoise hotel overlooking the sands, and the endless line of run-down motels with their grimy little lamps, their graffiti-covered walls. The first waves, already frequented by a few insomniac surfers, the oh-so-melancholy palm trees with their Roaring Twenties grace, and the merry-go-round. The bay that bends round towards Long Beach is as vast as the Bay of Ipanema in Rio, the only one of comparable size. But, unlike Rio with its proud, luxurious, and pretentious (though none the less beautiful) sea front, here the town ends almost in a piece of wasteground at the ocean, like a seaside suburb. And it has indeed the hazy charm of just such a suburb. Here at dawn, it is one of the most insignificant shorelines in the world, just a place to go fishing. The Western World ends on a shore devoid of all signification, like a journey that loses all meaning when it reaches its end. The immense metropolis of Los Angeles peters out here in the sea like a desert, with all the nonchalance of a desert.

'LIVE OR DIE': the graffiti message on the pier at Santa Monica is mysterious, because we really have no choice between life and death. If you live, you live, if you die, you die. It is like saying 'be yourself, or don't be!' It is stupid, and yet it is enigmatic. You could read it to mean that you should live intensely or else disappear, but that is banal. Following the model of 'pay or die!', 'your money or your life!', it would become 'your life or your life!'. Stupid again, since you cannot exchange life for itself. And yet there is poetic force in this implacable tautology, as there always is when there is nothing to be understood. In the end, the lesson of this graffiti is perhaps: 'if you get more stupid than me, you die!'

Where the others spend their time in libraries, I spend mine in the deserts and on the roads. Where they draw their material from the history of ideas, I draw mine from what is happening now, from the life of the streets, the beauty of nature. This country is naive, so you have to be naive. Everything here still bears the marks of a primitive society: technologies, the media, total simulation (bio-, socio-, stereo-, video-) are developing in a wild state, in their original state. Insignificance exists on a grand scale and the desert remains the primal scene, even in the big cities. Inordinate space, a simplicity of language and character . . .

My hunting grounds are the deserts, the mountains, Los Angeles, the freeways, the Safeways, the ghost towns, or the downtowns, not lectures at the university. I know the deserts, their deserts, better than they do, since they turn their backs on their own space as the Greeks turned their backs on the sea, and I get to know more about the concrete, social life of America from the desert than I ever would from official or intellectual gatherings.

American culture is heir to the deserts, but the deserts here are not part of a Nature defined by contrast with the town. Rather they denote the emptiness, the radical nudity that is the background to every human institution. At the same time, they designate human institutions as a metaphor of that emptiness and the work of man as the continuity of the desert, culture as a mirage and as the perpetuity of the simulacrum.

The natural deserts tell me what I need to know about the deserts of the sign. They teach me to read surface and movement and geology and immobility at the same time. They create a vision expurgated of all the rest: cities, relationships, events, media. They induce in me an exalting vision of the desertification of signs and men. They form the mental frontier where the projects of civilization run into the ground. They are outside the sphere and circumference of desire. We should always appeal to the deserts against the excess of signification, of intention and pretention in culture. They are our mythic operator.

*Romero Saddle – Camino Cielo – Blue
Canyon – Quick Silver Mine – Sycamore
Canyon – San Rafael Wilderness*

As night is falling, after three hours driving, I am lost in the San Rafael Wilderness. Driving on and on towards the last of the sun's rays, then by the headlights reflecting in the sand of the river bed. Will I get through or won't I? Darkness is falling all around: the prospect of spending the night here looms, but the whisky creates a delicious sense of abandon. At last, after two hours driving and a descent into hell, I am resurrected in heaven, on the Camino Cielo ridge, with an aerial, night-time view of the lights of Santa Barbara.

Porterville

The journey here through forests of orange trees, their leaves a deep, geometric green, laid out neatly on wild hillsides that are carpeted with undulating grass like animal fur and resemble the hills of Tuscany. A driveway lined by fifty palm trees, all the same height and absolutely symmetrical, leads up to a planter's house that is minuscule by comparison. All its shutters are closed. It could be a colonial scene, but in fact these are the western slopes of the Rockies, at the foot of Sequoia National Park. The road down into this town that is not really a town is as straight as the rows of orange trees and is peopled by Mexican slaves who have bought up their masters' old 1950s Chevrolets. You go down through an oleander-lined avenue. But the real revelation is the town itself, which is completely devoid – to a point unintelligible to us Europeans – of any centre. You drive up and down every street in the town without being able to find anything remotely like a central point. Without even a bank, an administrative building, or a town hall, the town has no coordinates; it is like a plantation. The only sign of life: an American flag, just alongside the dead centre of the town, the hotel. This is the only three-storey building and its torn curtains flap through the broken window-panes in the warm late-afternoon wind. The hotel rooms can't even be opened. The Mexican owner can't find the keys. The prices are ridiculously low. You can spend a week here for twenty dollars. And yet in every room, with its sagging mattress and its dusty mirror, the TV is constantly on, apparently not for any resident, since it is on in the rooms that are open to the winds and those that can't even be opened. You can see the televisions, or at least their reflections, from the street, through the curtains. All the corridors, with their worn-out carpets, display a single sign: EXIT. You can leave in any direction you like. You can rent three rooms here for a week for the price of a night in an ordinary motel. Forty years ago, no doubt, it was a hotel for Bakersfield's smart set when they escaped to the cool of the mountains. Today it is the heart of

Porterville, and an irrevocable process of decay has set in. But it is too hot to worry about that.

Darkness falls slowly on Porterville, and Saturday night fever begins. 'American Graffiti 85.' All the cars drive up and down the main thoroughfare in slow or animated procession, a collective parade, drinking, eating ice-creams, calling out from one car to the next (whereas in the daytime they all drive round oblivious of anyone else). Music, PA systems, beer, ice-cream. It is the same ceremony, on a smaller scale, as the slow nocturnal cruising on the Strip in Las Vegas, or the procession of cars on the Los Angeles freeways simply transformed into a Saturday night provincial extravaganza. The only element of culture, the only mobile element: the car. No cultural centre, no centre of entertainment. A primitive society: the same motor identification, the same collective phantasy of an unfolding ritual – breakfast, movie, religious service, love and death – the whole of life as a drive-in. Truly magnificent. It is all in this parade of bulky capsules, luminous and silent (the whole thing passes off in relative silence with no gear changes and no overtaking; these are the same fluid monsters with their automatic transmissions, gliding along smoothly one behind the other). Nothing else will happen during the evening. Except that is for the madcap race between the 12–15-year-old girls – like cowgirls from a Western – which takes place in a corner of the town, under floodlights, in the dust kicked up by the horses, near the baseball park. And the next morning, Sunday morning, the deserted streets, streets hardly distinct from the desert, have a preternatural calm about them. The air is transparent, with the orange trees all around. After the night's automobile ceremony the town is abandoned now to the light of its over-wide avenues, the lifeless stores, the half-awake service stations. Natural, orphaned light, without headlights or advertising signs. Just a few Mexicans cruise around in their long cars, while the first Whites wash theirs in front of their open verandas. The luminous insignificance of Sunday morning. A holographic micro-model of all America.

Death Valley is as big and mysterious as ever. Fire, heat, light: all the elements of sacrifice are here. You always have to bring something into the desert to sacrifice, and offer it to the desert as a victim. A woman. If something has to disappear, something matching the desert for beauty, why not a woman?

Nothing is more alien to American deserts than symbiosis (loose-fitting clothing, slow rhythms, oases) such as you find in native desert cultures. Here, everything human is artificial. Furnace Creek is a synthetic, air-conditioned oasis. But there is nothing more beautiful than artificial coolness in the midst of heat, artificial speed in the middle of a natural expanse, electric light under a blazing sun, or the artificial practice of gambling in lost casinos. Reyner Banham is right: Death Valley and Las Vegas are inseparable; you have to accept everything at once, an unchanging timelessness and the wildest instantaneity. There is a mysterious affinity between the sterility of wide open spaces and that of gambling, between the sterility of speed and that of expenditure. That is the originality of the deserts of the American West; it lies in that violent, electric juxtaposition. And the same applies to the whole country: you must accept everything at once, because it is this telescoping that gives the American way of life its illuminating, exhilarating side, just as, in the desert, everything contributes to the magic of the desert. If you approach this society with the nuances of moral, aesthetic, or critical judgement, you will miss its originality, which comes

precisely from its defying judgement and pulling off a prodigious confusion of effects. To side-step that confusion and
excess is simply to evade the challenge it throws down to
you. The violence of its contrasts, the absence of discrimination between positive and negative effects, the telescoping
of races, technologies, and models, the waltz of simulacra
and images here is such that, as with dream elements, you
must accept the way they follow one another, even if it seems
unintelligible; you must come to see this whirl of things and
events as an irresistible, fundamental datum.

The distinctions that are made elsewhere have little meaning here. It would be misguided to focus on aspects of an
American civility that is often in fact far superior to our own
(in our land of 'high culture') and then to point out that in
other respects the Americans are barbarians. It would be
wrong-headed to counterpose Death Valley, the sublime
natural phenomenon, to Las Vegas, the abject cultural
phenomenon. For the one is the hidden face of the other and
they mirror each other across the desert, the one as acme of
secrecy and silence, the other as acme of prostitution and
theatricality.

Having said that, there is something mysterious about
Death Valley *in itself*. However beautiful the deserts of
Utah and California may be, this one is something else
again – something sublime. The preternatural heat haze
that enshrouds it, its inverse depth – below sea level – this
landscape with its underwater features, its salt surfaces and
mudhills, the high mountain chains surrounding it, making it
a kind of inner sanctuary – a gentle, spectral place of initiation (which comes from its geological depth and the atmosphere of spiritual limbo). What has always struck me about
Death Valley is its *mildness*, its pastel shades and its fossil

veil, the misty fantasmagoria of its mineral opera. There is nothing funereal or morbid about it: a transverberation in which everything is palpable, the mineral softness of the air, the mineral substance of the light, the corpuscular fluid of the colours, the total extraversion of one's body in the heat. A fragment of another planet (at least predating any form of human life), where another, deeper temporality reigns, on whose surface you float as you would on salt-laden waters. The senses, the mind, and even your sense of belonging to the human race are all numbed by the fact of having before you the pure, unadulterated sign of 180 million years, and therefore the implacable enigma of your own existence. It is the only place where it is possible to relive, alongside the physical spectrum of colours, the spectrum of the inhuman metamorphoses that preceded us, our successive historical forms: the mineral, the organic, salt desert, sand dunes, rock, ore, light, heat, everything the earth has been, all the inhuman forms it has been through, gathered together in a single anthologizing vision.

The desert is a natural extension of the inner silence of the body. If humanity's language, technology, and buildings are an extension of its constructive faculties, the desert alone is an extension of its capacity for absence, the ideal schema of humanity's disappearance. When you come out of the Mojave, writes Banham, it is difficult to focus less than fifteen miles ahead of you. Your eye can no longer rest on objects that are near. It can no longer properly settle on things, and all the human or natural constructions that intercept your gaze seem irksome obstacles which merely corrupt the perfect reach of your vision. When you emerge from the desert, your eyes go on trying to create emptiness all around; in every inhabited area, every landscape they see desert beneath, like a watermark. It takes a long time to get back to a normal vision of things and you never succeed completely. Take this substance from my sight! ... But the desert is more than merely a space from which all substance has been removed. Just as silence is not what remains when all noise has been suppressed. There is no need to close your eyes to hear it. For it is also the silence of time.

And even the foreshortening effect of cinema is present in Death Valley, for all this mysterious geology is also a scenario. The American desert is an extraordinary piece of drama, though in no sense is it theatrical like an Alpine land-scape, nor sentimental like the forest or the countryside. Nor eroded and monotonous like the sub-lunar Australian desert. Nor mystical like the deserts of Islam. It is purely, geologi-cally dramatic, bringing together the sharpest, most ductile shapes with the gentlest, most lascivious underwater forms – the whole metamorphism of the earth's crust is present in synthesis, in a miraculous abridged version. All the intelli-gence of the earth and its elements gathered together here, in a matchless spectacle: a geological epic. Cinema is not alone in having given us a cinematic vision of the desert. Nature itself pulled off the finest of its special effects here, long before men came on the scene.

It is useless to seek to strip the desert of its cinematic aspects in order to restore its original essence; those features are thoroughly superimposed upon it and will not go away. The cinema has absorbed everything – Indians, *mesas*, canyons, skies. And yet it is the most striking spectacle in the world. Should we prefer 'authentic' deserts and deep oases? For us moderns, and ultramoderns, as for Baudelaire, who knew that the secret of true modernity was to be found in artifice, the only natural spectacle that is really gripping is the one which offers both the most moving profundity *and at the same time the total simulacrum of that profundity*. As here, where the depth of time is revealed through the (cinematic) depth of field. Monument Valley is the geology of the earth, the mausoleum of the Indians, and the camera of John Ford. It is erosion and it is extermination, but it is also the tracking shot, the movies. All three are mingled in the vision we have of it. And each phase subtly terminates the preceding one. The extermination of the Indians put an end to the natural cosmological rhythm of these landscapes, to which their magical existence was bound for millennia. With the arrival of pioneer civilization an extremely slow process gave way to a much quicker one. But this process itself was overtaken fifty years later by the tracking shots of the cinema which speeded up the process even more and, in a sense, put an end to the disappearance of the Indians by reviving them as extras. Thus this landscape has been witness to all the great events both of geology and anthropology, including some of the most recent. Hence the exceptional scenic qualities of the deserts of the West, combining as they do the most ancestral of hieroglyphs, the most vivid light, and the most total superficiality.

Colours there seem rarefied, detached from all substance, diffracted into the air, floating on the surface of things. Hence the spectral, ghostly, and at the same time veiled, translucent, calm, and subtle impression made by these landscapes. And the mirage effect – a temporal mirage too – which comes near to total illusion. The rocks, sands, crystals, and cacti are eternal, but they are also ephemeral, unreal, and detached from their substance. The vegetation is minimal, but indestructible, and each new spring sees a miracle of bloom. By contrast, light itself has substance here. Floating like a powder on the air, it gives all shades of colour that pastel nuance that seems the very image of disincarnation, of the separation of the body from the spirit. In this sense, one may speak of the abstraction of the desert, of a deliverance from the organic, a deliverance that is beyond the body's abject passage into carnal inexistence, into that dry, luminous phase of death in which the corruption of the body reaches completion. The desert is beyond this accursed phase of decomposition, this humid phase of the body, this organic phase of nature.

The desert is a sublime form that banishes all sociality, all sentimentality, all sexuality. Words, even when they speak of the desert, are always unwelcome. Caresses have no meaning, except from a woman who is herself of the desert, who has that instantaneous, superficial animality in which the fleshly is combined with dryness and disincarnation. And yet, in another sense, there is nothing to match night falling in its shroud of silence on Death Valley, seen from broken-down, worn-out motel chairs on the veranda, looking out over the dunes. The heat does not fall off here. Only night falls, its darkness pierced by a few car headlights. And the silence is something extraordinary, as though it were itself all ears. It is not the silence of cold, nor of barrenness, nor of an absence of life. It is the silence of the whole of this heat over the mineral expanses that stretch out before us for hundreds of miles, the silence of the gentle wind upon the salt mud of Badwater, caressing the ore deposits of Telegraph Peak. A silence internal to the Valley itself, the silence of underwater erosion, below the very waterline of time, as it is below the level of the sea. No animal movement. Nothing dreams here, nothing talks in its sleep. Each night the earth plunges into perfectly calm darkness, into the blackness of its alkaline gestation, into the happy depression of its birth.

Long before I left, I could not get Santa Barbara out of my mind. Santa Barbara is simply a dream and it has in it all the processes of dreams: the wearisome fulfilment of all desires, condensation, displacement, facility of action. All this very quickly becomes unreal. Happy days! This morning a bird came to my balcony to die. I photographed it. But no one is indifferent to his own life and the least event still has something moving about it. I was here in my imagination long before I actually came here. Suddenly this stay has become a sojourn in a previous existence. In the last weeks, time seemed multiplied by a feeling of no longer being there and of living Santa Barbara each day, with its fatal charm and its blandness, as the predestined site of an eternal return.

Things fade into the distance faster and faster in the rear-view mirror of memory. Two and a half months disappear in a few moments, even quicker than the jet lag when your mind readjusts to Europe. It's not easy keeping your sense of wonderment alive or the first flashes of surprise, or even recalling what it felt like when things were still unexpected. Things last no longer than the time it takes for them to happen. It used to be the agreeable custom that you went to see the same film more than once. We are losing that habit. I doubt now whether we really see our whole life flashing before us at the moment of our death. The very possibility of the Eternal Return is becoming precarious: that marvellous perspective presupposes that things unfold in a necessary, predestined order, the sense of which lies beyond them.

There is nothing like that today; things merely follow on in a flabby order that leads nowhere. Today's Eternal Return is that of the infinitely small, the fractal, the obsessive repetition of things on a microscopic and inhuman scale. It is not the exaltation of a will, nor the sovereign affirmation of an event, nor its consecration by an immutable sign, such as Nietzsche sought, but the viral recurrence of microprocesses. This is, admittedly, inescapable, but no powerful sign presents it to the imagination as predestined (neither nuclear explosions nor viral implosions can be *named* by the imagination). Such are the events which surround us: microprocessive and instantaneously obliterated.

Coming back from California means re-entering a world you have known and lived in, but doing so without feeling the charm you might expect at returning to a former life. You had left that world behind in the hope it might be thoroughly transformed in your absence, but nothing of the sort has occurred. It got along quite nicely without you and it adjusts quite smoothly to your return. People and things conspire to make it seem as if you had not been away. For my own part, I left it all without regrets and I come back to it again without any great emotion. People are a thousand times more preoccupied with their own little lives than with the strangeness of another world. You are best advised, then, to land discreetly, to come back politely into this world keeping anything you may have to say – along with the few sights still gleaming in your memory – strictly to yourself.

The confrontation between America and Europe reveals not so much a *rapprochement* as a distortion, an unbridgeable rift. There isn't just a gap between us, but a whole chasm of modernity. You are born modern, you do not become so.

And we have never become so. What strikes you immediately in Paris is that you are in the nineteenth century. Coming from Los Angeles, you land back in the 1800s. Every country bears a sort of historical predestination, which almost definitively determines its characteristics. For us, it is the bourgeois model of 1789 – and the interminable decadence of that model – that shapes our landscape. There is nothing we can do about it: everything here revolves around the nineteenth-century bourgeois dream.

Utopia Achieved

For the European, even today, America represents something akin to exile, a phantasy of emigration and, therefore, a form of interiorization of his or her own culture. At the same time, it corresponds to a violent extraversion and therefore to the zero degree of that same culture. No other country embodies to the same extent both this function of disincarnation and, at the same time, the functions of exacerbation and radicalization of the elements of our European cultures . . . It is by an act of force or *coup de théâtre* – the geographical exile of the Founding Fathers of the seventeenth century adding itself to the voluntary exile of man within his own consciousness – that what in Europe had remained a critical and religious esotericism became transformed on the New Continent into a pragmatic exotericism. The whole foundation of America is a response to this dual operation of a deepening of the moral law in individual consciences, a radicalization of the utopian demand which was always that of the sects, and the immediate materialization of that utopia in work, custom, and way of life. To land in America is, even today, to land in that 'religion' of the way of life which Tocqueville described. This material utopia of the way of life, where success and action are seen

as profound illustrations of the moral law, was crystallized
by exile and emigration and these have, in a sense, transformed it into a primal scene. For us, in Europe, it was the
Revolution of 1789 that set its seal upon us, though it was
a different seal, that of History, the State, and Ideology.
Politics and history, not the utopian, moral sphere, remain
our primal scene. And if this 'transcendent' European-style
revolution is far from confident today either of its means or
its ends, the same cannot be said of the immanent revolution
of the American way of life, of that moral and pragmatic
assertiveness which constitutes now as ever the pathos of
the New World.

America is the original version of modernity. We are the
dubbed or subtitled version. America ducks the question of
origins; it cultivates no origin or mythical authenticity; it has
no past and no founding truth. Having known no primitive
accumulation of time, it lives in a perpetual present. Having
seen no slow, centuries-long accumulation of a principle of
truth, it lives in perpetual simulation, in a perpetual present
of signs. It has no ancestral territory. The Indians' territory is
today marked off in reservations, the equivalent of the galleries in which America stocks its Rembrandts and Renoirs. But
this is of no importance – America has no identity problem.
In the future, power will belong to those peoples with no
origins and no authenticity who know how to exploit that
situation to the full. Look at Japan, which to a certain extent
has pulled off this trick better than the US itself, managing,
in what seems to us an unintelligible paradox, to transform
the power of territoriality and feudalism into that of deterri-
toriality and weightlessness. Japan is already a satellite of the
planet Earth. But America was already in its day a satellite of

the planet Europe. Whether we like it or not, the future has shifted towards artificial satellites.

The US is utopia achieved.

We should not judge their crisis as we would judge our own, the crisis of the old European countries. Ours is a crisis of historical ideals facing up to the impossibility of their realization. Theirs is the crisis of an achieved utopia, confronted with the problem of its duration and permanence. The Americans are not wrong in their idyllic conviction that they are at the centre of the world, the supreme power, the absolute model for everyone. And this conviction is not so much founded on natural resources, technologies, and arms, as on the miraculous premiss of a utopia made reality, of a society which, with a directness we might judge unbearable, is built on the idea that it is the realization of everything the others have dreamt of – justice, plenty, rule of law, wealth, freedom: it knows this, it believes in it, and in the end, the others have come to believe in it too.

In the present crisis of values, everyone ends up turning towards the culture which dared to forge right ahead and, by a theatrical masterstroke, turn those values into reality, towards that society which, thanks to the geographical and mental break effected by emigration, allowed itself to imagine it could create an ideal world from nothing. We should also not forget the fantasy consecration of this process by the cinema. Whatever happens, and whatever one thinks of the arrogance of the dollar or the multinationals, it is this culture which, the world over, fascinates those very people who suffer most at its hands, and it does so through the deep, insane conviction that it has made all their dreams come true.

But this is really not so very crazy: all pioneer societies have been more or less ideal societies. Even the Jesuits of Paraguay. Even the Portuguese in Brazil founded what was in a sense an ideal patriarchal, slave-owning society, though unlike the American, Anglo-Saxon, Puritan model, the southern model had little chance of being universally adopted in the modern world. By exporting itself, by becoming hypostatized across the sea, the ideal purged itself of its history, took on concrete reality, developed with new blood and experimental energy. The dynamism of the 'new worlds' still bears witness to their superiority over the 'old countries': the ideal the others only cultivated as an ultimate, and secretly impossible, goal, they put into operation.

Colonization was, in this sense, a world-scale *coup de théâtre* which leaves deep, nostalgic traces everywhere, even when it is collapsing. For the Old World, it represents the unique experience of an idealized substitution of values, almost as you find in science-fiction novels (the tone of which it often reflects, as in the US), a substitution which at a stroke short-circuited the destiny of these values in their countries of origin. The emergence of these societies at the margins deprives the historical societies of their destinies. The brutal extrapolation of their essence across the seas means that they lose control of their development. They are eradicated by the ideal model they have themselves secreted. And development will never again take place in the form of progressive alignment. The moment at which those values, which up to then had been transcendent, are realized, are projected into reality, or collapse in the encounter with it (America), is an irreversible one. This is what separates us, come what may, from the Americans. We shall never catch them up, and we shall never have their candour. We merely imitate them, parody

them with a fifty-year time lag, and we are not even successful at that. We do not have either the spirit or the audacity for
what might be called the zero degree of culture, the power of
unculture. It is no good our trying more or less to adapt, their
vision of the world will always be beyond our grasp, just as
the transcendental, historical *Weltanschauung* of Europe will
always be beyond the Americans. Just as the countries of the
Third World will never internalize the values of democracy
and technological progress. There are some gaps that are
definitive and cannot be bridged.

We shall remain nostalgic utopians, agonizing over our
ideals, but baulking, ultimately, at their realization, profess-
ing that everything is possible, but never that everything has
been achieved. Yet that is what America asserts. Our problem is that our old goals – revolution, progress, freedom –
will have evaporated before they were achieved, before they
became reality. Hence our melancholy. We shall never have
had the good fortune to enjoy the *coup de théâtre*.

We live in negativity and contradiction; they live in paradox
(for a realized utopia is a paradoxical idea). And the quality of
the American way of life resides for many in that pragmatic,
paradoxical humour of theirs, whilst ours is (was?) characterized by the subtlety of our critical wit. Many American intellectuals envy us this and would like to fashion a set of ideal
values and a history for themselves, and relive the philosophical or Marxist delights of old Europe. Yet this runs against the
grain of everything that makes up their original situation, since
the charm and power of American (un)culture derive precisely
from the sudden and unprecedented materialization of models.

When I see Americans, particularly American intellectuals, casting a nostalgic eye towards Europe, its history, its

metaphysics, its cuisine, and its past, I tell myself that this is just a case of unhappy transference. History and Marxism are like fine wines and haute cuisine: they do not really cross the ocean, in spite of the many impressive attempts that have been made to adapt them to new surroundings. This is a just revenge for the fact that we Europeans have never really been able to domesticate modernity, which also refuses to cross the ocean, though in the other direction. There are products which cannot be imported or exported. That is our loss – and theirs. If, for us, society is a carnivorous flower, history for them is an exotic one. Its fragrance is no more convincing than the bouquet of Californian wines (in spite of all the effort being expended to make us believe otherwise).

Not only can history not be caught up, but it seems that in this 'capitalist' society capital can never actually be grasped in its present reality. It is not that our Marxist critics have not tried to run after it, but it always stays a length ahead of them. By the time one phase has been unmasked, capital has already passed on to another (Ernest Mandel and his third phase of world capital). Capital cheats. It doesn't play by the rules of critique, the true game of history. It eludes the dialectic, which only reconstitutes it after the event, a revolution behind. Even anti-capitalist revolutions only serve to give fresh impetus to its own: they are the equivalent of the 'exogenous events' Mandel speaks of, like wars, crises, or the discovery of goldmines, which set capital off on a new developmental process on fresh bases. In the end, these theorists themselves reveal the inanity of their hopes. By reinventing capital in each successive phase on the basis of the primacy of political economy, they simply confirm the absolute initiative capital enjoys as historical event. They therefore fall straight into their own trap and give themselves no chance of getting ahead of it. And this at the same time ensures – as was perhaps their objective – the continuing validity of their retrospective analyses.

America has never been short of violence, nor of events, people, or ideas, but these things do not of themselves constitute a history. Octavio Paz is right when he argues that America was created in the hope of escaping from history, of building a utopia sheltered from history, and that it has in part succeeded in that project, a project it is still pursuing today. The concept of history as the transcending of a social and political rationality, as a dialectical, conflictual vision of societies, is not theirs, just as modernity, conceived precisely as an original break with a certain history, will never be ours. We have lived long enough now in the unhappy consciousness of this modernity to be aware of that. Europe invented a certain kind of feudalism, aristocracy, bourgeoisie, ideology, and revolution: all this had meaning for us, but at bottom it had no meaning elsewhere. All who have tried to ape these things have either made themselves a laughing stock or have been dramatically driven off course (we ourselves are doing little more than merely imitating ourselves, outliving ourselves). America made a break with all that and found itself in a situation of radical modernity: it is, therefore, in America and nowhere else that modernity is original. We can only imitate it without being able to challenge it on its own home territory. Once an event has taken place, it has taken place, full stop. And when I see Europe casting longing eyes towards all-out modernity, I tell myself that that, too, is an unhappy transference.

We are still at the centre, but at the centre of the Old World. They who were a marginal transcendence of that

Old World are today its new, eccentric centre. Eccentricity is stamped on their birth certificate. We shall never be able to take it from them. We shall never be able to excentre or decentre ourselves in the same way. We shall therefore never be modern in the proper sense of the term. And we shall never enjoy the same freedom – not the formal freedom we take for granted, but the concrete, flexible functional, active freedom we see at work in American institutions and in the head of each citizen. Our conception of freedom will never be able to rival their spatial, mobile conception, which derives from the fact that at a certain point they freed themselves from that historical centrality.

From the day when that eccentric modernity was born in all its glory on the other side of the Atlantic, Europe began to disappear. The myths migrated. Today, all the myths of modernity are American. It will do us no good to worry our poor heads over this. In Los Angeles, Europe has disappeared. As Isabelle Huppert says: 'They have everything. They don't need anything. Admittedly, they envy us our past and our culture and admire them, but deep down to them we are a sort of elegant Third World.' In the political sphere, there will always remain of this initial decentring a federalism, an absence of centralism and, at the level of mores and culture, a decentralization, an eccentricity which is that of the New World in relation to Europe. The US has no insoluble problem of federation (they have, of course, had their War of Secession, but we are speaking here of the current federal set-up), because they are from the outset, from the very dawn of their history, a culture of mixing, of national and racial mix, of rivalry and heterogeneity. This is clearly visible in New York where each successive skyscraper and, after its own fashion, each ethnic group has dominated the city, and where the whole none the less still gives the impression not of a heteroclite mish-mash, but of converging energies, not of unity or plurality, but of intensity born of rivalry, of antagonistic power, thus creating a complicity, a collective attraction, beyond culture or politics, in the very violence or banality of the way of life.

If we stay with this line of thinking, we can see that there is a profound difference in racial, ethnic tone between America and France. In America the violent mixing of multiple European nationalities, then of exogenous races, produced an original situation. This multiracialism transformed the country and gave it its characteristic complexity. In France there was neither an initial mix, nor a real resolution, nor was there any real challenge between ethnic groups. All that happened was a transferring of the colonial situation back to the metropolis, out of its original context. All our immigrants are, at bottom, *harkis*,* living under the social protection of their oppressors, to whom they can oppose only their poverty and their de facto sentence of transportation for life. Immigration is, admittedly, a hot issue, but the presence of several million immigrants has not made its mark on the French way of life nor changed the face of the country. That is why, when you return to France, the dominant impression is a clammy sense of petty racism, of everyone being in an awkward, shameful position. The sequel to a colonial situation, in which the bad faith of both colonizer and colonized persists, whereas in America, each ethnic group, each race develops a language, a culture in competition with and sometimes superior to that of the 'natives', and each group

---

* *Harkis* are Algerian Muslims who took French citizenship after Algerian Independence. [Tr.]

symbolically rises to the top. This is not a question of formal equality or freedom, but of a de facto freedom expressed in rivalry and competition and this gives a singular vivacity and an air of openness to the confrontation between the races.

Our European culture is one that has staked its all on the universal and the danger menacing it is that of perishing by the universal . . . This includes not only the extension of the concepts of market, monetary exchange, or production goods, but also the imperialism of the idea of culture. We should be wary of this idea, which has, like the concept of revolution, only become universal by being abstractly formalized, and which devours singularity just as rapidly as revolution devours its children.

One consequence of this claim to universality is that it makes both downward diversification and upward federation equally impossible. Once a nation and a culture have been centralized by a solid historical process, they experience insurmountable difficulties when they attempt either to create viable sub-units or to integrate themselves into some coherent larger entity . . . There is a sort of inevitability about the centralizing process. Hence the difficulties currently being encountered in the attempt to find a European spirit and culture, a European dynamism. Inability to produce a federal event (Europe), a local event (decentralization), a racial event (multiracialism). Too entangled by our history, we can only produce an apologetic centralism (a *Clochemerle* pluralism) and an apologetic mixing (our soft racism).

The principle of achieved utopia explains the absence and, moreover, the lack of need for metaphysics and the imaginary in American life. It gives Americans a perception of reality different from our own. The real is not connected with the impossible and no failure can throw it into question. What is thought in Europe becomes reality in America – everything that disappears in Europe reappears in San Francisco!

And yet the idea of an achieved utopia is a paradoxical one. If it is negativity, irony, and the sublime that govern European thinking, it is paradox which dominates that of America, the paradoxical humour of an achieved materiality, of an ever renewed self-evidence, of a bright new faith in the legality of the *fait accompli* which we always find amazing, the humour of a naive visibility of things, whilst we operate in the uncanny realm of the *déjà vu* and the glaucous transcendence of history.

We criticize Americans for not being able either to analyse or conceptualize. But this is a wrong-headed critique. It is we who imagine that everything culminates in transcendence, and that nothing exists which has not been conceptualized. Not only do they care little for such a view, but their perspective is the very opposite: it is not conceptualizing reality, but realizing concepts and materializing ideas, that interests them. The ideas of the religion and enlightened morality of the eighteenth century certainly, but also dreams, scientific values, and sexual perversions. Materializing freedom, but also the unconscious. Our phantasies around space and fiction, but also our phantasies of sincerity and virtue, or our mad dreams of technicity. Everything that has been dreamt on this side of the Atlantic has a chance of being realized on the other. They build the real out of ideas. We transform the real into ideas, or into ideology. Here in America only what is produced or manifested has meaning; for us in Europe only what can be thought or concealed has meaning. Even materialism is only an idea in Europe. It is in America that it becomes concretely realized in the technical operation of things, in the transformation of a way of thinking into a way of life, in the 'action' of life ('action' in the film-making sense, as what happens when the cameras begin to roll). For the materiality of things is, of course, their cinematography.

Americans believe in facts, but not in facticity. They do not know that facts are factitious, as their name suggests. It is in this belief in facts, in the total credibility of what is done or seen, in this pragmatic evidence of things and an accompanying contempt for what may be called appearances or the play of apperances – a face does not deceive, behaviour does not deceive, a scientific process does not deceive, nothing deceives, nothing is ambivalent (and at bottom this is true: nothing deceives, there are no lies, *there is only simulation*, which is precisely the facticity of facts) – that the Americans are a true utopian society, in their religion of the *fait accompli*, in the naivety of their deductions, in their ignorance of the evil genius of things. You have to be utopian to think that in a human order, of whatever nature, things can be as plain and straightforward as that. All other societies contain within them some heresy or other, some dissidence, some kind of suspicion of reality, the superstitious belief in a force of evil and the possible control of that force by magic, a belief in the power of appearances. Here, there is no dissidence, no suspicion. The emperor has no clothes; the facts are there before us. As is well known, the Americans are fascinated by the yellow-skinned peoples in whom they sense a superior form of cunning, a higher form of that absence of truth which frightens them.

Admittedly, the irony of community is missing here, as is the playfulness of social life. The charm to be found in social graces and in the theatre of social relations is all transferred outwards into the advertising of life and lifestyles. This is a society that is endlessly concerned to vindicate itself, perpetually seeking to justify its own existence. Everything has to be made public: what you are worth, what you earn, how you live – there is no place here for interplay of a subtler nature. The society's 'look' is a self-publicizing one. The American flag itself bears witness to this by its omnipresence, in fields and build-up areas, at service stations, and on graves in the cemeteries, not as a heroic sign, but as the trademark of a good brand. It is simply the label of the finest successful international enterprise, the US. This explains why the hyperrealists were able to paint it naively, without either irony or protest (Jim Dine in the sixties), in much the same way as Pop Art gleefully transposed the amazing banality of consumer goods on to its canvases. There is nothing here of the fierce parodying of the American anthem by Jimi Hendrix, merely the light irony and neutral humour of things that have become banal, the humour of the mobile home and the giant hamburger on the sixteen-foot-long billboard, the pop and hyper humour so characteristic of the atmosphere of America, where things almost seem endowed with a certain indulgence towards their own banality. But they are indulgent towards their own craziness too. Looked at more generally, they do not lay claim to being extraordinary; they simply are extraordinary. They have that extravagance which makes up odd, everyday America. This oddness is not surrealistic (surrealism is an extravagance that is still aesthetic in nature and as such very European in inspiration); here, the extravagance has passed into things. Madness, which with us is subjective, has here become objective, and irony which is subjective with us has also turned into something objective. The fantasmagoria and excess which we locate in the mind and the mental faculties have passed into things themselves.

Whatever the boredom, the hellish tedium of the everyday in the US or anywhere else, American banality will always be a thousand times more interesting than the European – and especially the French – variety. Perhaps because banality here is born of extreme distances, of the monotony of wide-open spaces and the radical absence of culture. It is a native flower here, as is the opposite extreme, that of speed and verticality, of an excess that verges on abandon, and indifference to values bordering on immorality, whereas French banality is a hangover from bourgeois everyday life, born out of a dying aristocratic culture and transmuted into petty-bourgeois mannerism as the bourgeoisie shrank away throughout the nineteenth century. This is the crux: it is the corpse of the bourgeoisie that separates us. With us, it is that class that is the carrier of the chromosome of banality, whereas the Americans have succeeded in preserving some humour in the material signs of manifest reality and wealth.

This also explains why Europeans experience anything relating to statistics as tragic. They immediately read in them their individual failure and take refuge in a pained denunciation of the merely quantitative. The Americans, by contrast, see statistics as an optimistic stimulus, as representing the dimensions of their good fortune, their joyous membership of the majority. Theirs is the only country where quantity can be extolled without compunction.

This same indulgence and humour which things attest in their banality here, Americans also show towards themselves and other people. Their intellectual conduct is pleasant, a model of gentleness. They make no claim to what we call intelligence and they do not feel threatened by other people's. For them, this is merely a particular cast of mind in which one should not indulge unduly. They do not therefore move spontaneously to deny or contest; their natural inclination is towards agreement. When we say 'I agree with you', we do so to contest what follows. When an American says he agrees, it is because, in all honesty, he can see no reason to demur. But quite often he will confirm your analysis by facts, statistics, or lived experience, thereby divesting it of all conceptual value.

This self-indulgence, which is not without humour, is evidence of a society secure in its wealth and power, a society which seems, to some extent, to have internalized Hannah Arendt's comment that the American revolution, unlike the European revolutions, was successful. But even a successful revolution has its victims and its sacrificial emblems. When all is said and done, it is on the murder of Kennedy that Reagan's current reign is founded. That murder has been neither avenged nor elucidated, and with good reason. And this is not to mention the murder of the Indians. It is the energy of Kennedy's murder which radiates out over present-day America. I say this to illustrate not only the indulgence, but the self-publicizing, self-justificatory violence of this society, that triumphalist violence which forms part of all successful revolutions.

Tocqueville describes the beneficial effects of democracy and the American constitution with considerable enthusiasm, praising the inherent freedom of the way of life, the regularity of mores (rather than the equality of status), the supremacy of a moral (rather than political) organization of society. He then describes with equal lucidity the extermination of the Indians and the condition of the Negroes, without ever bringing these two realities together. As if good and evil had developed separately. Is it possible that one can, while keenly feeling both these aspects, pass over the relation between them? Certainly it is, and the same paradox faces us today: *we shall never resolve the enigma of the relation between the negative foundations of greatness and that greatness itself.* America is powerful and original; America is violent and abominable. We should not seek to deny either of these aspects, nor reconcile them.

But what has become of this paradoxical grandeur, the New World's original situation as described by Tocqueville? What has become of this American revolution that consisted in the dynamic resolution of a clearly understood individual interest and a well-tempered collective morality? A problem that was not resolved in Europe and for that reason was to fuel a problematic of history, of the State, and the disappearance of the State, which America has not known. What has become of the challenge sketched out in Tocqueville: can a nation strike a pact of greatness on the basis of each individual's banal interest alone? Can there exist a pact of equality and banality (of interests, rights, and wealth) which retains a heroic and original dimension? (for what is a society without a heroic dimension?). In short, has the New World fulfilled its promise? Has it reaped the benefits of freedom to the full, or has it merely garnered all the unhappy consequences of equality?

The glory of American power is most often described as an effect of freedom and its exercise. But freedom does not of itself generate power. Freedom understood as public action, as the collective discourse of a society on its own undertakings and values, has in fact disappeared in the individual liberation of mores and in agitation (agitation, as is well known, is one of the Americans' main activities). It is, therefore, equality and its consequences that have been more instrumental in the creation of power. This is the equality of which Tocqueville once said, in a fine phrase, 'I do not find fault with equality for drawing men into the pursuit of forbidden pleasures, but for absorbing them entirely in the search for the pleasures that are permitted.' It is this equality, the modern equalization of statuses and values, the uniformity of features and characters, which gives birth to power. It is around this equality that Tocqueville's paradox is recast: the American world tends both towards absolute insignificance (all things tending to become equal and therefore cancelling each other out in their power) and towards absolute originality – today even more than 150 years ago, the effects having been multiplied by geographical extension. *This is a world that has shown genius in its irrepressible development of equality, banality, and indifference.*

It is this overall dynamism, this dynamic of the abolition of differences which is so exciting and which poses, in Tocqueville's words, a new problem for the understanding of human societies. It is, moreover, extraordinary to see how little the Americans have changed in the last two centuries – much less than European societies. Whereas these were caught up in the revolutions of the nineteenth century, the Americans kept intact – preserved as it was by a breadth of ocean that created something akin to temporal insularity – the utopian and moral perspective of the men of the eighteenth century, or even of the Puritan sects of the seventeenth, transplanted and kept alive, safely sheltered from the vicissitudes of history. This Puritan and moral hysteresis is that of exile, that of utopia. We criticize them for this: why did the revolution not take place here, in this new country, this land of liberty and advanced bastion of capitalism? Why do the 'social' and the 'political', our favoured categories, have so little purchase here? The answer is that the social and philosophical nineteenth century did not cross the Atlantic and here the driving forces are utopia and morality, the concrete idea of happiness and mores, all of which political ideology, with Marx at its head, liquidated in Europe in favour of an 'objective' conception of historical transformation. It is from this point of view that we tax Americans with historical naivety and moral hypocrisy. But the fact is simply that, in their collective consciousness, they are closer to the models of thought of the eighteenth century, which are utopian and pragmatic, than to those that were to be imposed by the French revolution, which were ideological and revolutionary.

Why are the sects so powerful and dynamic? The mixing of races, institutions, and technologies should have swept them away long ago. Yet the fact is that they have preserved here the living form and practical illuminism of their origins, together with their moral obsession. In a sense, it is their micro-model which has been extended to the whole of America. From the beginning, the sects played the major role in the move towards an achieved utopia, which is the equivalent of an 'acting out'. They it is who live on utopia (the Church considers it a virtual heresy) and who strive to bring about the Kingdom of God on Earth, whereas the Church restricts itself to the hope of salvation and theological virtues.

It is as though America as a whole had espoused this sect-like destiny: the immediate concretization of all perspectives of salvation. The multiplication of individual sects should not fool us: the important point is that the whole of America is preoccupied with the sect as a moral institution, with its immediate demand for beatification, its material efficacity, its compulsion for justification, and doubtless also with its madness and frenzy.

If America were to lose this moral perspective on itself, it would collapse. This is not perhaps evident to Europeans, for whom America is a cynical power and its morality a hypocritical ideology. We remain unconvinced by the moral vision Americans have of themselves, but in this we are wrong. When they ask with such seriousness why other peoples detest them, we would be wrong to smile, for it is this same self-examination which makes possible both the various 'Watergates' and the unrelenting exposure of corruption and their own society's faults in the cinema and the media, a freedom we might envy them, we who are the truly hypocritical societies, keeping our individual and public affairs concealed beneath the bourgeois affectations of secrecy and respectability.

Tocqueville's central idea is that the spirit of America is to be found in its mode of life, in the revolution of mores, the moral revolution. This creates neither a new legality nor a new State, but it does create a practical legitimacy, a legitimacy grounded in the way of life. Salvation no longer has to do with the divine or the State, but with the ideal form of practical organization. Is this to be traced back to the secularization of conscience effected by Protestantism, to the introjection of divine jurisdiction into daily discipline? The fact is that religion has become part of everyday life, which means that it can no longer be challenged or questioned as to its bases, since it no longer has transcendent value. This is religion as way of life. Similarly, politics has become part of everyday life – as pragmatic machine, as game, as interaction, as spectacle – which means that it can no longer be judged from a specifically political point of view. There is no ideological or philosophical principle of government any more. Things are at once both more naive and more conjunctural. This does not mean there are no strategies, but they are modal, not final strategies. Sexuality itself has become part of life, which means that it, too, no longer has transcendent value, neither as prohibition, nor as principle of analysis, pleasure, or transgression. It has been 'ecologized', psychologized, secularized for domestic use. It has become part of the way of life.

The pre-eminent position accorded to mores, the hegemony enjoyed by the 'way of life' signifies that the abstract universal of law is subordinated to the concrete regulation of exchanges. Law is not consensual: you are supposed to know it and obey it. But there may be honour in disobeying it too, and history is made of the simultaneous extolling of the law and of those who have broken it. What strikes you, by contrast, in the American system, is that there is no honour in breaking laws, nor prestige in transgression or being exceptional. This is that notorious American conformism, which we see as a sign of social and political weakness. But the fact is that people are more united on concrete regulation than on abstract legislation here; they are more agreed on informal ways of doing things than on a formal authority. What could it mean to dissociate oneself from a rule, to challenge a mechanism? You have to understand this conventional, pragmatic solidarity of American customs, which is based not on a social contract but on a kind of moral pact, and which might be compared not so much to the highway code, which anyone may disobey, as to the consensus that governs driving on the freeways. This conformity makes American society close to primitive societies, in which it would be absurd to distinguish oneself morally by disobeying the collective ritual. American conformism is not therefore 'naive': it is the product of a pact at the level of custom, of a set of rules and procedures which presuppose quasispontaneous adherence. Whereas our lives, by contrast, are governed by an equally ritualized disobedience of our own value system.

This 'conformism' reflects a particular kind of freedom: the absence of prejudice and pretentiousness. One might suggest that Americans' lack of prejudice has to do with their lack of judgement. This would be unfair, but all things considered why should we not prefer that lightfooted solution to our heavy, pretentious one? Just look at this girl who serves you in the guest-room: she does so *in total freedom*, with a smile, without prejudice or pretentiousness, as though she were sitting opposite you. The situation is not an equal one, but she does not pretend to equality. Equality is part of the way of life here. Precisely the opposite of Sartre's waiter, who is completely alienated from his representation and who only resolves the situation by calling on a theatrical metalanguage, by affecting in his gestures a freedom and an equality he does not really enjoy. Hence the unhappy intellectualism of his behaviour, which is shared, in our part of the world, by almost all social classes. This question of equality in mores, of freedom in mores has neither been resolved nor even properly posed within our culture. Only the political or philosophical question of equality has been posed and that keeps us locked in our eternal pretentiousness. In America – and this is a commonplace – you are astonished by the almost natural way status is forgotten, by the ease and freedom of personal relations. This ease may seem banal or vulgar to us, but it is never ridiculous. It is *our* affectation which is ridiculous.

You only have to see a French family settling in on a Californian beach to feel the abominable weight of our culture. The American group remains open; the French unit immediately creates a closed space. The American child roams far and wide; the French one hovers around its parents. The Americans see to it that they stay well stocked with ice and beer; the French see to it that social niceties are observed, and that they keep up a theatrical show of well-being. People move around a lot on American beaches; the Frenchman stays camped on his little sandy domain. The Frenchman makes quite a show on holiday, but the mediocrity of his petty-bourgeois space stays with him. Now, you can say anything you like about Americans, but they are neither mediocre nor petty-bourgeois. They certainly do not have aristocratic grace, but they have an ease that comes from space, the ease of those who have always had lots of space, and this makes up for a lack of manners or noble breeding. The freedom of bodily movement which this possession of space gives them easily compensates for the blandness of their features and character. Vulgar but 'easy'. We are a culture of intimacy, which produces manners and affectation; they have a democratic culture of space. We are free in spirit, but they are free in their actions. The American moving around in the deserts or the national parks does not give the impression of being on holiday. Moving around is his natural occupation; nature is a frontier and a place for action. There is none of the flabby Romanticism and gallo-roman quietude that clutter up our free time. Nothing of the 'holiday' label, as it was invented in France by the Popular Front: the demoralizing atmosphere of free time snatched from the State, to be consumed in a plebeian spirit, with theatrical regard for one's hard-earned leisure. Freedom here has no static or negative definition. Its definition is spatial and mobile.

The great lesson of all this is that freedom and equality, like ease and grace, only exist where they are present from the outset. This is the surprise democracy had in store for us: equality is at the beginning, not at the end. That is the difference between egalitarianism and democracy: democracy presupposes equality at the outset, egalitarianism presupposes it at the end. Or, as Roger Price notes, 'Democracy demands that all of its citizens *begin* the race even. Egalitarianism insists that they all *finish* even.'

However, when the obsession with judging others or with social prejudices has been left behind, there is greater tolerance, but greater indifference too. No longer wishing others to see them, Americans end up not seeing one another. So people pass in the street without looking at one another, which may seem a mark of discretion and civility, but which is also a sign of indifference. At least this is not affected. It is both a quality and the absence of a quality.

When I speak of the American 'way of life', I do so to emphasize its utopian nature, its *mythic* banality, its dream quality, and its grandeur. That philosophy which is immanent not only in technological development but also in the exceeding of technology in its own excessive play, not only in modernity, but in the extravagance of modern forms (whether it be the vertical network of New York or the horizontal one of Los Angeles), not only in banality, but in the apocalyptic forms of banality, not only in the reality of everyday life, but in the hyperreality of that life which, as it is, displays all the characteristics of fiction. It is this fictional character which is so exciting. Now, fiction is not imagination. It is what anticipates imagination by giving it the form of reality. This is quite opposite to our own natural tendency which is to anticipate reality by imagining it, or to flee from it by idealizing it. That is why we shall never inhabit true fiction; we are condemned to the imaginary and to nostalgia for the future. The American way of life is spontaneously fictional, since it is a transcending of the imaginary in reality.

Fiction is not abstraction either, and if America suffers from a kind of infirmity when it comes to abstraction, that incapacity takes on a glory all its own in the sprawling reality of middle America, in the apotheosis of daily life, in that empirical genius which so amazes us. Perhaps this successful revolution is no longer successful in the way Tocqueville understood it, as a spontaneous movement of the public mind, a form of spontaneous, concrete ordering of mores to modern values. It is not so much in the operation of institutions as in the freeing of technologies and images that the glorious form of American reality is to be found: in the immoral dynamic of images, in the orgy of goods and services, an orgy of power and useless energy (yet who can say where useful energy ends?), in which the spirit of advertising is more to the fore than Tocqueville's public spirit. But these are, after all, the marks of its liberation, and the very obscenity of this society is the sign of its liberation. A liberation of *all effects*, some of them perfectly excessive and abject. But this is precisely the point: the high point of liberation, its logical outcome, is to be found in the spectacular orgy, speed, the instantaneity of change, generalized eccentricity. Politics *frees itself* in the spectacle, in the all-out advertising effect; sexuality frees itself in all its anomalies and perversions (including the refusal of sexuality, the latest fad, which is itself only a supercooling effect of sexual liberation); mores, customs, the body, and language free themselves in the ever quickening round of fashion. The liberated man is not the one who is freed in his ideal reality, his inner truth, or his transparency; he is the man who changes spaces, who circulates, who changes sex, clothes, and habits according to fashion, *rather than morality*, and who changes opinions not as his conscience dictates but in response to opinion polls. This is practical liberation whether we like it or not, whether or not we deplore its wastefulness and its obscenity. Moreover, people in 'totalitarian' countries know very well that this is true freedom and dream of nothing but fashion, the latest styles, idols, the play of images, travel for its own sake, advertising, the deluge of advertising. In short, the orgy. Now, you have to admit that it is America which has concretely, technologically achieved this orgy of liberation, this orgy of indifference, disconnection, exhibition, and circulation. I do not know what remains of the successful revolution Tocqueville speaks of, the revolution of political freedom and of the quality of public spirit (in this regard America today has both the best and the worst to offer), but it has certainly achieved *this revolution*, whereas we, having failed in our historical revolutions, our abstract revolutions, are in the process of failing in this other revolution too. We absorb these logical consequences of modernity, of this life-style revolution with all its inevitable excesses, in spite of ourselves, in homeopathic doses, with a mixture of fascination and resentment. We in Europe are stuck in the old rut of worshipping difference; this leaves us with a great handicap when it comes to radical modernity, which is founded on the absence of difference. Only very reluctantly do we become modern and in-different. This is why our own modernity is so lacklustre. This is why our undertakings lack the modern spirit. We do not even have the *evil genius* of modernity, that genius which pushes innovation to the point of extravagance and in so doing rediscovers a kind of fantastical liberty.

Everything that has been heroically played out and destroyed in Europe in the name of Revolution and Terror has been realized in its simplest, most empirical form on the other side of the Atlantic (the utopia of wealth, rights, freedom, the social contract, and representation). Similarly, everything we have dreamed in the radical name of anti-culture, the subversion of meaning, the destruction of reason and the end of representation, that whole anti-utopia which unleashed so many theoretical and political, aesthetic and social convulsions in Europe, without ever actually becoming a reality (May '68 is one of the last examples) has all been achieved here in America in the simplest, most radical way. *Utopia has been achieved here and anti-utopia is being achieved*: the anti-utopia of unreason, of deterritorialization, of the indeterminacy of language and the subject, of the neutralization of all values, of the death of culture. America is turning all this into reality and it is going about it in an uncontrolled, empirical way. All we do is dream and, occasionally, try and act out our dreams. America, by contrast, draws the logical, pragmatic consequences from everything that can possibly be thought. In this sense, it is naive and primitive; it knows nothing of the irony of concepts, nor the irony of seduction. It does not ironize upon the future or destiny: it gets on with turning things into material realities. To our utopian radicalism it counterposes its empirical radicalism, to which it alone gives dramatically concrete form. We philosophize on the end of lots of things, but it is here that they actually come to an end. It is here, for example, that territory has ceased to exist (though there is indeed a vast amount of space), here that the real and the imaginary have come to an end (opening all spaces up to simulation). It is here, therefore, that we should look for the ideal type of the end of our culture. It is the American way of life, which we think naive or culturally worthless, which will provide us with a complete graphic representation of the end of our values – which has vainly been prophesied in our own countries – on the grand scale that the geographical and mental dimensions of utopia can give to it.

But is this really what an achieved utopia looks like? Is this a successful revolution? Yes indeed! What do you expect a 'successful' revolution to look like? It is paradise. Santa Barbara is a paradise; Disneyland is a paradise; the US is a paradise. Paradise is just paradise. Mournful, monotonous, and superficial though it may be, it is paradise. There is no other. If you are prepared to accept the consequences of your dreams – not just the political and sentimental ones, but the theoretical and cultural ones as well – then you must still regard America today with the same naive enthusiasm as the generations that discovered the New World. That same enthusiasm which Americans themselves show for their own success, their own barbarism, their own power. If not, you have no understanding of the situation, and you will not be able to understand your own history – or the end of your history – either, because Europe can no longer be understood by starting out from Europe itself. The US is more mysterious: *The mystery of American reality* exceeds our fictions and our interpretations. The mystery of a society which seeks to give itself neither meaning nor an identity, which indulges neither in transcendence nor in aesthetics and which, *for precisely that reason*, invents the only great modern verticality in its buildings, which are the most grandiose manifestations within the vertical order and yet do not obey the rules of transcendence, which are the most prodigious pieces of architecture and yet do not obey the laws of aesthetics, which are ultra-modern and ultra-functional, but also have about them something non-speculative, primitive, and savage – a culture (or unculture) like this remains a mystery to us.

We are at home with introversion and reflexion and with different effects of meaning coexisting under the umbrella of a concept. But the object freed from its concept, free to deploy itself in extraverted form, in the equivalence of all its effects . . . To us this is a total enigma. Extraversion is a mystery to us in exactly the same way as the commodity was to Marx: the commodity, hieroglyph of the modern world, mysterious precisely because it is extraverted, a form realizing itself in its pure operation and in pure circulation (hello Karl!).

In this sense, for us the whole of America is a desert. Culture exists there in a wild state: it sacrifices all intellect, all aesthetics in a process of literal transcription into the real. Doubtless the original decentring into virgin territory gave it this wildness, though it certainly acquired it without the agreement of the Indians whom it destroyed. The dead Indian remains the mysterious guarantor of these primitive mechanisms, even into the modern age of images and technologies. Perhaps the Americans, who believed they had destroyed these Indians, merely disseminated their virulence. They have opened up the deserts, threaded and criss-crossed them with their freeways, but by some mysterious interaction their towns and cities have taken on the structure and colour of the desert. They have not destroyed space; they have simply rendered it infinite by the destruction of its centre (hence these infinitely extendable cities). In so doing, they have opened up a true fictional space. In the 'savage mind', too, there is no natural universe, no transcendence of either man or nature, or of history. Culture is everything, or nothing, depending on how you look at it. You find this same absence of distinction between the two in modern simulation. There is no natural universe there either, and you cannot differentiate between a desert and a metropolis. It is not that the Indians were infinitely close to nature, nor that the Americans are infinitely distant from it: both belong to the ideality of nature, as they do to the ideality of culture, and both are also equally alien to nature and culture.

There is no culture here, no cultural discourse. No ministries, no commissions, no subsidies, no promotion. There is none of the sickly cultural pathos which the whole of France indulges in, that fetishism of the cultural heritage, nor of our sentimental – and today also statist and protectionist – invocation of culture. The Beaubourg would be impossible here, just as it would in Italy (for other reasons). Not only does centralization not exist, but the idea of a cultivated culture does not exist either, no more than that of a theological, sacred religion. No culture of culture, no religion of religion. One should speak rather of an 'anthropological' culture, which consists in the invention of mores and a way of life. That is the only interesting culture here, just as it is New York's streets and not its museums or galleries that are interesting. Even in dance, cinema, the novel, fiction, and architecture, there is something wild in everything specifically American, something that has not known the glossy, high-flown rhetoric and theatricality of our bourgeois cultures, that has not been kitted out in the gaudy finery of cultural distinction.

Here in the US, culture is not that delicious panacea which we Europeans consume in a sacramental mental space and which has its own special columns in the newspapers – and in people's minds. Culture is space, speed, cinema, technology. This culture is authentic, if anything can be said to be authentic. This is not cinema or speed or technology as optional extra (everywhere in Europe you get a sense of modernity as something tacked on, heterogeneous, anachronistic). In America cinema is true because it is the whole of space, the whole way of life that are cinematic. The break between the two, the abstraction which we deplore, does not exist: life is cinema.

That is why searching for works of art or sophisticated entertainment here has always seemed tiresome and out of place to me. A mark of cultural ethnocentrism. If it is the lack of culture that is original, then it is the lack of culture one should embrace. If the term taste has any meaning, then it commands us not to export our aesthetic demands to places where they do not belong. When the Americans transfer Roman cloisters to the New York Cloysters, we find this unforgivably absurd. Let us not make the same mistake by transferring our cultural values to America. We have no right to such confusion. In a sense, they do because they have space, and their space is the refraction of all others. When Paul Getty gathers Rembrandts, Impressionists, and Greek statues together in a Pompeian villa on the Pacific coast, he is following American logic, the pure baroque logic of Disneyland. He is being original; it is a magnificent stroke of cynicism, naivety, kitsch, and unintended humour – something astonishing in its nonsensicality. Now the disappearance of aesthetics and higher values in kitsch and hyperreality is fascinating, as is the disappearance of history and the real in the televisual. It is in this unfettered pragmatics of values that we should find some pleasure. If you simply remain fixated on the familiar canon of high culture, you miss the essential point (which is, precisely, the inessential).

The advertisements which cut into the films on TV are admittedly an outrage, but they aptly emphasize that most television productions never even reach the 'aesthetic' level and are, basically, of the same order as advertisements. Most films – including many of the better ones – are made up from the same everyday romance: cars, telephones, psychology, make-up. They are purely and simply illustrations of the way of life. Advertising does just the same: it canonizes the way of life through images, making the whole a genuinely integrated circuit. And if everything on television is, without exception, part of a low-calorie (or even no-calorie) diet, then what good is it complaining about the adverts? By their worthlessness, they at least help to make the programmes around them seem of a higher level.

Banality, lack of culture, and vulgarity do not have the same meaning here as they have in Europe. Or perhaps this is merely the crazy notion of a European, a fascination with an unreal America. Perhaps Americans are quite simply vulgar, and this meta-vulgarity is merely something I have dreamt up. Who knows? But I am inclined to suggest, in time-honoured fashion, that you have nothing to lose if I am wrong and everything to gain if I am right. The fact is that a certain banality, a certain vulgarity which seem unacceptable to us in Europe seem more than acceptable – even fascinating – to us here. The fact is that all our analyses in terms of alienation, conformism, standardization, and dehumanization collapse of themselves: when we look at America it is the analyses which seem vulgar.

Why is a passage like the following (by G. Faye) both true and, at the same time, absolutely false?

California shines out as the total myth of our times. . . . Multiracialism, hegemonic technology, shrink-culture narcissism, urban criminality and audiovisual saturation: as super-America, California stands out as the absolute antithesis of authentic Europe . . from Hollywood to disco-pap, from *ET* to *Star Wars*, from the pseudo-rebellious itchings on the campuses to the ravings of Carl Sagan, from the neo-gnostics of Silicon Valley to the wind-surfing mystics, from the neo-Indian gurus to aerobics, from jogging to psychoanalysis as a form of democracy, from criminality as a form of psychoanalysis to television as an instrument of despotism, California has set itself up as the world centre of the simulacrum and the inauthentic, as the absolute synthesis of 'cool' Stalinism. An *hysterical* land; focus and meeting-place for the rootless, California is the land of non-history, of the non-event, but at the same time the site of the constant swirl, the uninterrupted rhythm of fashion, that is to say, the site of tremors going nowhere, those tremors which so obsess it, constantly threatened as it is by earthquakes.

California has invented nothing: it has taken everything from Europe and served it up again in a disfigured, meaningless form, with an added Disneyland glitter. World centre of sweet madness, mirror of our dejecta and our decadence. Californitis, that hot variant of Americanism, is unleashing itself on the young of today and emerging as a mental form of AIDS. . . . To the revolutionary *angst* of the Europeans, California counterposes its long procession of fakes: the parody of science on the rite-less campus, the parody of cities and urbanism in the sprawl of Los Angeles, the parody of technology in Silicon Valley, the parody of oenology in its insipid Sacramento wines, the parody of religion in its gurus and sects, the parody of eroticism in its beach boys,

the parody of drugs in its acids [?], the parody of sociability in its 'communities' . . . . Even nature in California is a
Hollywood parody of ancient Mediterranean landscapes:
a sea that is too blue [!?], mountains that are too rugged, a
climate that is too gentle or too arid, an uninhabited disenchanted nature, deserted by the gods: a sinister land beneath
a sun that is too bright. The expressionless face of our death,
since Europe will surely die sunburnt and smiling, with its
skin lightly baking under a holiday sun.

All this is true (if you like), since the text itself resembles
the hysterical stereotype it confers upon California. And it
is surely easy to detect in Faye's writing a degree of fascination with his subject. But if we could use precisely the same
terms to say exactly the opposite of what he says, then this
only emphasizes the point that, for his part, G. Faye was not
able to effect this same reversal. He has not grasped how, at
the edges of this meaningless world, this 'sweet madness' of
meaninglessness, this soft, air-conditioned hell he describes,
things turn into their opposites. He has not grasped the challenge of this 'marginal transcendence' in which precisely a
whole universe is brought up against its margins, its 'hysterical' simulation – and why not? Why should Los Angeles
not be a parody of cities? Why should Silicon Valley not
parody technology? Why should there not be a parody of
sociability, eroticism, and drugs, or even indeed a parody of
the (too blue!) sea and the (too bright!) sun. Not to mention
museums and culture. Of course all this is parody! If none of
these values can bear to be parodied, it must mean they no
longer have any importance. Yes, California (and America
with it) is the mirror of *our* decadence, but *it* is not decadent
at all. It is hyperreal in its vitality, it has all the energy of

the simulacrum. 'It is the world centre of the inauthentic.' Certainly it is: that is what gives it its originality and power. The irresistible rise of the simulacrum is something you can simply feel here without the slightest effort. But has he ever been here? If he had, he would know that the key to Europe is not to be found in its past history, but in this crazy, parodic anticipation that is the New World. He cannot see that even though every detail of America may be abject or insignificant, it is the whole which passes our imagining – by the same token, every detail in his description may be accurate, but it is the whole which goes beyond the bounds of stupidity.

What is new in America is the clash of the first level (primitive and wild) and the 'third kind' (the absolute simulacrum). There is no second level. This is a situation we find hard to grasp, since this is the one we have always privileged: the self-reflexive, self-mirroring level, the level of unhappy consciousness. But no vision of America makes sense without this reversal of our values: it is Disneyland that is authentic here! The cinema and TV are America's reality! The freeways, the Safeways, the skylines, speed, and deserts – these are America, not the galleries, churches, and culture . . . Let us grant this country the admiration it deserves and open our eyes to the absurdity of some of our own customs. This is one of the advantages, one of the pleasures of travel. To see and feel America, you have to have had for at least one moment in some downtown jungle, in the Painted Desert, or on some bend in a freeway, the feeling that Europe had disappeared. You have to have wondered, at least for a brief moment, 'How can anyone be European?'

F 354390 005   7/30/87   WASHINGTON DC
RONALD PEAGAN POINTS TO A BANDAGE AFTER
HAVING A BASAL CELL CANCER REMOVED FROM HIS NOSE.
PHOTO: © DIANA WALKER / LIAISON AGENCY

The End of US Power?

The fifties were the real high spot for the US ('when things were going on'), and you can still feel the nostalgia for those years, for the ecstasy of power, when power held power. In the seventies power was still there, but the spell was broken. That was orgy time (war, sex, Manson, Woodstock). Today the orgy is over. The US, like everyone else, now has to face up to a soft world order, a soft situation. Power has become impotent.

But if America is now no longer the monopolistic centre of world power, this is not because it has lost power, but simply because there is no centre any more. It has, rather, become the orbit of an imaginary power to which everyone now refers. From the point of view of competition, hegemony, and 'imperialism', it has certainly lost ground, but from the exponential point of view, it has gained some: take the unintelligible rise of the dollar, for example, which bears no relation to any economic supremacy, or the fabulous apotheosis of New York, or even – and why not? – the world-wide success of *Dallas*. America has retained power, both political and cultural, but it is now power as a special effect.

In the image of Reagan, the whole of America has become Californian. Ex-actor and ex-governor of California that he is, he has worked up his euphoric, cinematic, extraverted, advertising vision of the artificial paradises of the West to all-American dimensions. He has introduced a system where the easy life exerts a kind of blackmail, reviving the original American pact of an achieved utopia. It seems in fact that the ideal combination described by Tocqueville has come apart: though Americans have maintained a keen sense of individual interest, they do not seem to have preserved a sense of a meaning that could be collectively given to their undertakings. Hence the current crisis, which is deep-seated and real, and whose likely outcome seems to be a shift towards the rehabilitation of a collective principle, a set of values that would orient behaviour in a virtually spontaneous way and could present itself as an ideal resultant of all the various forces in play. What we see here is the success of Reagan's illusionist effort to resurrect the American primal scene. 'America is back again.' Left brittle by the Vietnam War, which was as unintelligible to them as the irruption of little green men in a cartoon strip – and which, incidentally, they dealt with as though it were a cartoon, as something remote from them, a television war, with no understanding of the world's condemnation of their actions and only able to see their enemy, since they are the achieved utopia of goodness, as the achieved utopia of Evil, Communism – they have taken refuge in the tranquillity of the easy life, in a triumphal illusionism. This too is entirely Californian, for in reality it is not always sunny in California. You often get fog with the sun, or smog in Los Angeles. And yet you retain a sun-filled memory of the place, a sunny screen memory. This is what the Reagan mirage is like.

Americans are no keener than anyone else today to think about whether they believe in the merits of their leaders, or even in the reality of power. That would take them on to much too tricky ground. They prefer to act as though they believed in them, on condition that their belief is not taken too much for granted. Governing today means giving acceptable signs of credibility. It is like advertising and it is the same effect that is achieved – commitment to a scenario, whether it be a political or an advertising scenario. Reagan's is both at once. It is also successful.

Everything is in the credits. Now that society has been definitively turned into an enterprise, everything is in the synopsis of performance and enterprise, and its leaders must produce all the signs of the advertising 'look'. The slightest failing becomes unpardonable, since the whole nation would be diminished by it. Even illness can become part of this 'look', as for example with Reagan's cancer. By contrast, political weaknesses or stupidity are of no importance. Image alone counts.

This consensus around simulation is much less fragile than is commonly thought, since it is far less exposed to any testing against political truth. All our modern governments owe a kind of political meta-stability to the regulation of public opinion by advertising. Mistakes, scandals, and failures no longer signal catastrophe. The crucial thing is that they be made credible, and that the public be made aware of the efforts being expended in that direction. The 'marketing' immunity of governments is similar to that of the major brands of washing powder.

No one keeps count of the mistakes made by the world's political leaders any more, mistakes which, in days gone by, would have brought about their downfall; no one much minds these now within our present system of simulation of government and of consensus through indifference. The people no longer take pride in their leaders and the leaders no longer pride themselves on their decisions. The tiniest bit of window-dressing is all that is needed to restore market confidence. Take, for example, the operation in Grenada, which followed the three hundred deaths in Lebanon: risk-free scenario, calculated production, artificial event – success ensured. And the two events, Lebanon and Grenada, bore witness to the same political unreality: the one, a terrorist act, was completely beyond control; the other, a total fake, was too much under control. Neither had any meaning so far as the art of government is concerned. Both were equally vacuous, as empty as today's political arena.

There is this same self-advertisement, this same cult of the credit titles in the new Reagan generation. Dynamic and euphoric, or rather generating dynamism and spreading euphoria. They see neither happiness as a new idea, nor success as a compelling one, since they already have all these things. They are not the militants of happiness and success, but its sympathizers. The generation that has come from the sixties and seventies, but has rid itself of all nostalgia for, all bad conscience about, and even any subconscious memory of those wild years. The very last traces of marginality excised as if by plastic surgery: new faces, new fingernails, glossy brain-cells, the whole topped with a tousle of software. A generation neither fired by ambition nor fuelled by the energy of repression, but completely refocused upon themselves, in love with business not so much for profit or prestige as for its being a sort of performance, a technical feat. They hover around the media, advertising, and computing.

They are not the ogres of business, but the footsloggers of showbiz, for business itself has become showbiz. 'Clean and perfect.' The Yuppies. Their joyous readaptation sings out in their very name. There has been no heart-rending reappraisal to separate them from the preceding generation, just an excision, an amnesia, an absolution – the mildly unreal process of forgetting that follows an event that is too intense to deal with. The Yuppies are not defectors from revolt, they are a new race, assured, amnestied, exculpated, moving with ease in the world of performance, mentally indifferent to any objective other than that of change and advertising (advertising everything: products, people, research, careers, lifestyle!). One might have expected the orgy of the sixties and seventies to throw up a mobile, disenchanted elite, but that has not been the case: the members of this elite, at least in their own publicity, see themselves as mobile and enchanted. Their enchantment takes mild forms: they are motivated, but not impassioned; whether in business, politics, or dataprocessing, they present themselves as cosily effective. Their slogan might well be:

> You can't have your money and spend it too!
> You can't have your cake and eat it too!
> You can't eat your wife and fuck it too!
> You can't live and have your living too!*

But this easy life knows no pity. Its logic is a pitiless one. If utopia has already been achieved, then unhappiness does not exist, the poor are no longer credible. If America is

---

* In English in original. [Tr.]

resuscitated, then the massacre of the Indians did not happen, Vietnam did not happen. While frequenting the rich ranchers or manufacturers of the West, Reagan has never had the faintest inkling of the poor and their existence, nor the slightest contact with them. He knows only the self-evidence of wealth, the tautology of power, which he magnifies to the dimensions of the nation, or indeed of the whole world. The have-nots will be condemned to oblivion, to abandonment, to disappearance pure and simple. This is 'must exit' logic: 'poor people must exit.' The ultimatum issued in the name of wealth and efficiency wipes them off the map. And rightly so, since they show such bad taste as to deviate from the general consensus.

That poverty which was until recently being relieved, which was still within the orbit of subsidized socialization, has all now fallen within the scope of providential (presidential) decree. It is as though the Last Judgment had already happened. The good have been found virtuous, the others have been cast out. No need for good will any more. No need to feel guilty. The Third World, which no one mourns, has been obliterated. After all, it only served to give the rich a bad conscience and all efforts to save it were certain to end in failure. That is all over. Long live the Fourth World, the world to which you can say, 'Right, utopia has arrived. If you aren't part of it, get lost!', the world that no longer has the right to surface, the disenfranchised, who have no voice and are condemned to oblivion, thrown out to go off and die their second-class deaths.

Disenfranchising.

You lose your rights one by one, first your job, then your car. And when your driver's licence goes, so does your identity. This way entire swathes of the population are falling into oblivion, being totally abandoned. Enfranchisement was an historical event: it was the emancipation of the serfs and slaves, the decolonization of the Third World and, in our societies, the various social and political rights: workers' rights, the vote, sexual liberation and the rights of women, prisoners and homosexuals – things which today have been won everywhere. Human rights have been won everywhere. The world is almost entirely liberated; there is nothing left to fight for. And yet at the same time entire social groups are being laid waste from the inside (individuals too). Society has forgotten them and now they are forgetting themselves. They fall out of all reckoning, zombies condemned to obliteration, consigned to statistical graphs of endangered species. This is the Fourth World. Entire sectors of our modern societies, entire countries in the Third World now fall into this Fourth World desert zone. But whereas the Third World still had a political meaning (even if it was a resounding world-wide failure), the Fourth World has none. It is transpolitical. *This is a result of our societies withdrawing political interest, of our advanced societies withdrawing social interest*, of that excommunication which affects precisely the communications-based societies. And it is true on a world scale. It can only be compared to the thousands of tons of coffee that were burnt in railway engines to keep up the world price. Or to those members of primitive tribes considered surplus to requirements who were led off like lemmings by some prophet, towards the ocean where they disappeared. The policies of governments are themselves becoming negative. They are no longer designed to socialize, to integrate, or to create new rights. Behind the appearance of socialization and participation they are desocializing, disenfranchising, and ejecting. The social order is contracting to include only economic exchange, technology, the sophisticated and innovative; as it intensifies these sectors, entire zones are 'disintensified', becoming reservations, and sometimes not even that: dumping grounds, wastelands, new deserts for the new poor, like the deserts you see forming around nuclear power stations or motorways. Nothing will be done to save them and perhaps nothing can be done, since enfranchisement, emancipation, and expansion have already taken place. There are therefore none of the elements here for a future revolution; what we see here are merely the inescapable results of an orgy of power, and an irreversible concentration of the world that has followed upon its extension. The only remaining question is this: what situation will result from this progressive disenfranchisement (which is already taking a violent turn under Reagan and Thatcher)?

Reagan's popularity gives us all food for thought. But we should first establish what type of confidence he is accorded. It is almost too good to be true. How can it be that every defence has fallen before him? How can it be that no mistake or political reversal damages his standing and that, paradoxically, his failures even improve it (which infuriates our French leaders, for whom things are the other way round: the more initiative and goodwill they show, the less popular they become). But the point is precisely that the confidence placed in Reagan is a *paradoxical confidence*. Just as we distinguish between real and paradoxical sleep, we should also distinguish between real and paradoxical confidence. The former is granted to a man or a leader on the basis of his qualities and his success. Paradoxical confidence is the confidence we place in someone *on the basis of their failure or their absence of qualities*. The prototype of this confidence is the failure of prophecy – a process that is well-known from the history of messianic and millenarian movements – following which the group, instead of denying its leader and dispersing, closes ranks around him and creates religious, sectarian, or ecclesiastical institutions to preserve the faith. Institutions all the more solid for deriving their energy from the failure of the prophecy. This 'supplemental' confidence never wavers, because it derives from the disavowal of failure. Such, making all due allowance, is the amazing aura that surrounds Reagan's credibility, and which necessarily makes one think that the American prophecy, the grand prospect of utopia on earth combined with world power, has suffered a setback; that something of that imaginary feat that was to crown the history of two centuries has precisely not been realized, and that Reagan is the product of the failure of that prophecy. In Reagan, a system of values that was formerly effective turns into something ideal and imaginary. The image of America becomes imaginary for Americans themselves, at a point when it is without doubt profoundly compromised. This transformation of spontaneous confidence into paradoxical confidence and an achieved utopia into an imaginary hyperbole seems to me to mark a decisive turning-point. But doubtless things are not this simple. For I am not saying that the image of America is deeply altered in the eyes of the Americans themselves. I am not saying that this change of direction in the Reagan era is anything other than an incidental development. Who knows? You have the same difficulty today distinguishing between a process and its simulation, for example between a flight and a flight simulation. America, too, has entered this era of undecidability: is it still really powerful or merely simulating power?

Can Reagan be considered the symbol of present-day

American society – a society which, having once possessed the original features of power, is now perhaps at the face-lift stage? Another hypothesis might be that America is no longer what it was, but is continuing on its course; its power has entered a phase of hysteresis. Hysteresis: the process whereby something continues to develop by inertia, whereby an effect persists even when its cause has disappeared. We may speak, in this sense, of a hysteresis of history, a hysteresis of socialism, and so on. The whole thing continues to function like a body in motion by virtue of the speed it has already gathered or by inertia-steering, or like an unconscious man still remaining on his feet, by sheer force of equilibrium. Or, in more comic vein, like the cyclist in Jarry's *Supermale*, who has died of exhaustion on the incredible trip across Siberia, but who carries on pedalling and propelling the Great Machine, his rigor mortis transformed into motive power. A superb fiction, for the dead are perhaps even capable of going quicker, of keeping the machine going better than the living *since they no longer have any problems*. Might America not be like Jarry's five-man bicycle? But here again, though it seems quite clear the American machine has suffered something like a break in the current, or a breaking of the spell, who can say whether this is the product of a depression or of a supercooling of the machinery?

America is certainly suffering less than Europe from the phase of convalescence that grand ideas are going through or from the decline in historical passions, for these are not the motor of its development. It is, however, suffering from the disappearance of ideologies that might contest its power and from the weakening of all the forces that previously opposed it. It was more powerful in the two decades after the Second World War, but so too were the ideas and passions ranged against it. The American system could be violently attacked (even from within in the sixties and seventies). Today, America no longer has the same hegemony, no longer enjoys the same monopoly, but it is, in a sense, uncontested and uncontestable. It used to be a world power; it has now become a model (business, the market, free enterprise, performance) – and a universal one – even reaching as far as China. The international style is now American. There is no real opposition any more; the combative periphery has now been reabsorbed (China, Cuba, Vietnam); the great anti-capitalist ideology has been emptied of its substance. All in all, the same consensus is forming around the US in the world at large as has developed around Reagan at home. A credibility effect, an advertising effect, the potential adversary losing its defences. This is the way things have gone for Reagan. Little by little, everything facing him, everything opposing him has faded away, without its being possible to credit him with any personal political genius. Consensus by effusion, by an elision of the oppositional elements and the margins. Political decline, but PR ascendancy. It's the same for the US on a planetary scale. American power does not seem inspired by any spirit or genius of its own (it works by inertia, in an ad hoc fashion, in the void, hampered by its own strength). Yet, on the other hand, the country indulges in a kind of promotional hype. America has a sort of mythical power throughout the world, a power based on the advertising image, which parallels the polarization of advertising images around Reagan. It is in this way, by this kind of added value, of exponential, self-referential, though ultimately unfounded credibility, that an entire society becomes stabilized beneath a perfusion of advertising. The flooding of the dollar on the world marketplace is the symbol and finest example of this.

Yet it is a fragile meta-stability, as much externally as on the domestic political stage. For, in the last resort, it is due to the evaporation of any real alternative, to the disappearance of resistances and antibodies. This is the real crisis of American power, that of a potential stabilization by inertia, of an assumption of power in a vacuum. In many respects it resembles the loss of immune defences in an overprotected organism. That is why I feel there is a poetic irony in Reagan contracting cancer. In its form, cancer is somewhat similar to that transparent credibility, that euphoria of a body no longer producing antibodies and threatened with destruction by an excess of functionality. The leader of the greatest world power struck down by cancer! Power in the grip of metastases! The two poles of our civilization meet here. The end of presidential immunity. It will be AIDS next! This should mark the beginning of a general implosion (in the Eastern bloc, political power has long been in the grip of necrosis).

But we are going a bit quickly; we should perhaps rather speak of a menopause. An abatement of the fever in the public mind, a general realignment after the convulsions of the seventies, no more 'new frontiers', a conservative image-conscious management of things, steady, unambitious performativity with no thought of the future, austerity and physical training, business and jogging, the end of the mad whirl and the orgy, the restoration of a sort of naturalist utopia of the enterprise and a bio-sociological conservation of the race – does all this signify the end of the glories of potency, and the onset of the hysterical euphoria of the menopause? Or, once again, is the Reagan phase merely a temporary period of convalescence, a revival after a breakdown, but one presaging further developments. Yet no 'new frontier', no new 'Kennedy philosophy' seems thinkable today. Indeed, that is what has changed so profoundly in the atmosphere of America: the Reagan effect has sapped the nation's energy.

Having said that, this menopause effect is not peculiar to America. It can be seen in all the Western democracies and it is wreaking its havoc everywhere, in culture as well as in politics, in individual emotions and in ideological passions. One can only hope that as we enter that third phase that is old age, we shall also see some close encounters of the third kind (we have already known the debauched excess of middle age – fascism). As for American reality, even the face-lifted variety retains its vast scope, its tremendous scale, and, at the same time, an unspoilt rawness. All societies end up wearing masks. Why not the mask of Reagan? But what remains intact is what was there at the beginning: space and the spirit of fiction.

Desert for Ever

The sunsets are giant rainbows lasting for an hour. The seasons here make no sense: in the morning it is spring, at noon it is summer, and the desert nights are cold without it ever being winter. It is a kind of suspended eternity in which the year is renewed daily, with the guarantee that it will be like this each day, that every evening will be that rainbow of all the colours of the spectrum in which light, after having reigned all day long in its indivisible form, in the evening fragments into all the nuances of colour that make it up, before it finally disappears. Nuances which are already those of the instant rainbow catching fire in the wind on the crest of the Pacific waves.

This is the invulnerable grace of the climate, privilege of a nature that completes that insane richness that is man's.

This country is without hope. Even its garbage is clean, its trade lubricated, its traffic pacified. The latent, the lacteal, the lethal – life is so liquid, the signs and messages are so liquid, the bodies and the cars so fluid, the hair so blond, and the soft technologies so luxuriant, that a European dreams of death and murder, of suicide motels, of orgies and cannibalism to counteract the perfection of the ocean, of the light, of that insane ease of life, to counteract the hyperreality of every-thing here.

Hence the phantasy of a seismic fracture and a crumbling into the Pacific, which would be the end of California and of its criminal and scandalous beauty. For it is unbearable, while one is still alive, to pass beyond the difficulty of being, simply to pass into the fluidity of sky, cliffs, surf, and deserts, into the hypothesis of happiness alone.

But even the seismic challenge is still only a flirtation with death; it still forms part of the natural beauty, as do history or revolutionary theory, whose hyperrealist echoes come here to die with the discreet charm of something from a previous existence. All that remains of a violent and histori-cal demand is this graffiti on the beach, facing out to sea, no longer calling upon the revolutionary masses, but speaking to the sky and the open space and the transparent deities of the Pacific:

PLEASE, REVOLUTION!

And yet is it irrelevant that the largest naval base, that of the Pacific 7th Fleet – the very incarnation of American world-wide domination and the greatest firepower in the world – also contributes to this insolent beauty? In the very place where the beautiful magic of Santa Ana blows, the desert wind that crosses over the mountains to stay for four or five days, before scattering the fog, scorching the earth, making the sea sparkle, and crushing those who are used to the mist – the most beautiful thing about the Santa Ana is spending the night on the beach, swimming there as if it were daytime, and tanning, like vampires, under the moonlight.

This country is without hope.

We fanatics of aesthetics and meaning, of culture, of flavour and seduction, we who see only what is profoundly moral as beautiful and for whom only the heroic distinction between nature and culture is exciting, we who are unfailingly attached to the wonders of critical sense and transcendence find it a mental shock and a unique release to discover the fascination of nonsense and of this vertiginous disconnection, as sovereign in the cities as in the deserts. To discover that one can exult in the liquidation of all culture and rejoice in the consecration of in-difference.

I speak of the American deserts and of the cities which are not cities. No oases, no monuments; infinite panning shots over mineral landscapes and freeways. Everywhere: Los Angeles or Twenty-Nine Palms, Las Vegas or Borrego Springs . . .

No desire: the desert. Desire is still something deeply natural, we live off its vestiges in Europe, and off the vestiges of a moribund critical culture. Here the cities are mobile deserts. No monuments and no history: the exaltation of mobile deserts and simulation. There is the same wildness in the endless, indifferent cities as in the intact silence of the Badlands. Why is LA, why are the deserts so fascinating? It is because you are delivered from all depth there – a brilliant, mobile, superficial neutrality, a challenge to meaning and profundity, a challenge to nature and culture, an outer hyperspace, with no origin, no reference-points.

*   *   *

No charm, no seduction in all this. Seduction is elsewhere, in Italy, in certain landscapes that have become paintings, as culturalized and refined in their design as the cities and museums that house them. Circumscribed, traced-out, highly seductive spaces where meaning, at these heights of luxury, has finally become adornment. It is exactly the reverse here: there is no seduction, but there is an absolute fascination – the fascination of the very disappearance of all aesthetic and critical forms of life in the irradiation of an objectless neutrality. Immanent and solar. The fascination of the desert: immobility without desire. Of Los Angeles: insane circulation without desire. The end of aesthetics.

It is not just the aesthetics of decor (of nature or architecture) that vanishes into thin air, but the aesthetics of bodies and language, of everything that forms the European's – especially the Latin European's – mental and social *habitus*, that continual *commedia dell'arte*, the pathos and rhetoric of social relations, the dramatization of speech, the subtle play of language, the aura of make-up and artificial gesture. The whole aesthetic and rhetorical system of seduction, of taste, of charm, of theatre, but also of contradictions, of violence always reappropriated by speech, by play, by distance, by artifice. Our universe is never desert-like, always theatrical. Always ambiguous. Always cultural, and faintly ridiculous in its hereditary culturality.

What is arresting here is the absence of all these things – both the absence of architecture in the cities, which are nothing but long tracking shots of signals, and the dizzying absence of emotion and character in the faces and bodies. Handsome, fluid, supple, or cool, or grotesquely obese, probably less as a result of compulsive bulimia than a general incoherence, which results in a casualness about the body or language, food or the city: a loose network of individual, successive functions, a hypertrophied cell tissue proliferating in all directions.

Thus the only tissue of the city is that of the freeways, a vehicular, or rather an incessant transurbanistic, tissue, the extraordinary spectacle of these thousands of cars moving at the same speed, in both directions, headlights full on in broad daylight, on the Ventura Freeway, coming from nowhere, going nowhere: an immense collective act, rolling along, ceaselessly unrolling, without aggression, without objectives – transferential sociality, doubtless the only kind in a hyperreal, technological, soft-mobile era, exhausting itself in surfaces, networks, and soft technologies. No elevator or subway in Los Angeles. No verticality or underground, no intimacy or collectivity, no streets or facades, no centre or monuments: a fantastic space, a spectral and discontinuous succession of all the various functions, of all signs with no hierarchical ordering – an extravaganza of indifference, extravaganza of undifferentiated surfaces – the power of pure open space, the kind you find in the deserts. The power of the desert form: it is the erasure of traces in the desert, of the signified of signs in the cities, of any psychology in bodies. An animal and metaphysical fascination – the direct fascination of space, the immanent fascination of dryness and sterility.

The mythical power of California consists in this mixture of extreme disconnection and vertiginous mobility captured in the setting, the hyperreal scenario of deserts, freeways, ocean, and sun. Nowhere else does there exist such a stunning fusion of a radical lack of culture and natural beauty, of the wonder of nature and the absolute simulacrum: *just in this mixture of extreme irreferentiality and deconnection overall, but embedded in most primeval and great-featured natural scenery of deserts and ocean and sun — nowhere else is this antagonistic climax to be found.*

Elsewhere, sites of natural beauty are heavy with meaning, with nostalgia, and the culture itself is unbearable in its seriousness. The strong cultures (Mexico, Japan, Islam) reflect back to us the image of our degraded one, and the image of our profound guilt. The surplus of meaning in a strong, ritual, territorial culture turns us into gringos, zombies, tourists kept under house arrest in the country's natural beauty spots.

No such thing in California, where there is total rigour, for culture itself is a desert there, and culture has to be a desert so that everything can be equal and shine out in the same supernatural form.

This is why even the flight from London to Los Angeles, passing over the pole, is, in its stratospheric abstraction and its hyperreality, already part of California and the deserts. Deterritorialization begins with the disconnection of night and day. When their division is no longer a matter of time, but of space, altitude, and speed, and occurs cleanly, as if vertically, when you pass through the night as if it were a cloud, so fast that you can see it, as if it were a nearby object

*   Italicized section in English in original. [Tr.]

revolving around the earth, or, by contrast, when it is reduced to nothing, the sun remaining at the same point in the sky for all twelve hours of the flight, then this already marks the end of our space-time, that same enchanted reality which will be that of the West.

The wonder of the heat is metaphysical. The very colours – pastel blue, mauve, lilac – are the products of a slow, geological, timeless combustion. The mineral quality of the earth breaks through the surface in the crystalline flora. All the natural elements here have known their ordeal by fire. The desert is no longer a landscape, it is a pure form produced by the abstraction of all others.

Its definition is absolute, its frontier initiatory, its ridges steep, its contours cruel. It is a place of signs of an imperious necessity, an ineluctable necessity – but void of all meaning, arbitrary and inhuman, and one crosses it without deciphering them. Irrevocable transparency. The towns of the desert also end abruptly; they have no surround. And they have about them something of the mirage, which may vanish at any instant. You have only to see Las Vegas, sublime Las Vegas, rise in its entirety from the desert at nightfall bathed in phosphorescent lights, and return to the desert when the sun rises, after exhausting its intense, superficial energy all night long, still more intense in the first light of dawn, to understand the secret of the desert and the signs to be found there: a spellbinding discontinuity, an all-enveloping, intermittent radiation.

The secret affinity between gambling and the desert: the intensity of gambling reinforced by the presence of the desert all around the town. The air-conditioned freshness of the gaming rooms, as against the radiant heat outside. The challenge of all the artificial lights to the violence of the sun's rays. Night of gambling sunlit on all sides; the glittering darkness of these rooms in the middle of the desert. Gambling itself is a desert form, inhuman, uncultured, initiatory, a challenge to the natural economy of value, a crazed activity on the fringes of exchange. But it too has a strict limit and stops abruptly; its boundaries are exact, its passion knows no confusion. Neither the desert nor gambling are open areas; their spaces are finite and concentric, increasing in intensity toward the interior, toward a central point, be it the spirit of gambling or the heart of the desert – a privileged, immemorial space, where things lose their shadow, where money loses its value, and where the extreme rarity of traces of what signals to us there leads men to seek the instantaneity of wealth.

Picture Credits